TRUE TRUTH

Defending Absolute Truth in a Relativistic Age

ART LINDSLEY

InterVarsity Press
Downers Grove, Illinois

InterVarsity Press
P.O. Box 1400, Downers Grove, IL 60515-1426
World Wide Web: www.ivpress.com
E-mail: mail@ivpress.com

InterVarsity Press® *is the book-publishing division of InterVarsity Christian Fellowship/USA*®, *a student movement active on campus at hundreds of universities, colleges and schools of nursing in the United States of America, and a member movement of the International Fellowship of Evangelical Students. For information about local and regional activities, write Public Relations Dept., InterVarsity Christian Fellowship/USA, 6400 Schroeder Rd., P.O. Box 7895, Madison, WI 53707-7895, or visit the IVCF website at <www.ivcf.org>.*

All Scripture quotations, unless otherwise indicated, are taken from the New American Standard Version® (NASB). *All rights reserved.*

Design: Cindy Kiple

Images: Jens Lucking/Getty Images

ISBN 0-8308-3235-1

Printed in the United States of America ∞

Library of Congress Cataloging-in-Publication Data

Lindsley, Arthur William.
  True truth: defending absolute truth in a relativistic age/Arthur
Lindsley.
    p. cm.
  Includes bibliographical references.
  ISBN 0-8308-3235-1
  1. Truth—Religious aspects—Christianity. I. Title.
  BT50.L54 2004
  230'.01—dc22

                                                    2003027945

P	18	17	16	15	14	13	12	11	10	9	8	7	6	5	4	3
Y	19	18	17	16	15	14	13	12	11	10	09	08	07	06	05	04

I am incurably convinced that the object of opening the mind,
as of opening the mouth, is to shut it again on something solid.

G. K. CHESTERTON

To my sons,

Trey and Jonathan.

May you keep the belt of truth on tightly

and hold the sword of the Spirit,

the Word of God, in your hands.

CONTENTS

ACKNOWLEDGMENTS

I am indebted to many people as I write this book. First, I want to acknowledge Chuck Colson and the influence he has been on me not only personally but also through his books. It was, particularly, two *Breakpoint* editorials that provoked my thinking about the need to distinguish having a belief in absolutes from being an absolutist: "A Bad Rap: Why Christians Aren't Absolutists" and "Body of Christ: Who's an Absolutist" (*Breakpoint*, December 3, 1992). His emphasis put into words things I had been wrestling with for some time.

Second, I worked with R. C. Sproul for six years at the Ligonier Valley Study Center. Hearing him speak a few times each week during those years was a great treat. Much of my writing and teaching is marked by his influence. Third, Os Guinness was part of a summer program through the C. S. Lewis Institute for about ten years. Our Knowing and Doing conference lasted anywhere from two to five weeks. It was a pleasure hearing Os speak almost daily during those ten summers, and undoubtedly much of his way of thinking, cultural insights and terminology has influenced me. The notes I took then were lost long ago, but many things he said are etched in my memory. Fourth, Francis Schaeffer, from the time he spoke at my college chapel, pushed me to think harder and with a greater breadth.

In addition to the men listed above, there are many people to thank, particularly Becky Cooke, who prepared the manuscript through its many revisions. David Hazzard thoroughly edited the entire manuscript. Jim Beavers and Donald Drew read the manuscript carefully and gave many comments on content and style. Mike Marshall read the whole book at an early stage, giving his philosophical expertise and advice. Bill Nichels was one of the first readers of the roughest of drafts. Bill Cron gave some valuable input. Dave Brown urged me to put these thoughts into a book and helped along the way. Each one of these people helped improve the final product.

I also want to thank the staff and board of the C. S. Lewis Institute for their encouragement. The advisory board of my Oasis ministry provided encouragement and financial support to allow me the time to do this writing. I want to thank Doug and Nancy Greenwold, Jim and Becky Cooke, Todd and Pam Ramsey, Ken and Caroline Broussard, Kim and Kathy Cooke, Kerry and Deborah Moody, Jim and Lorraine Hiskey, and Bill and Marsha Nichels. I want to particularly thank Wayne and Wendy Hughes for their generous gift that gave us freedom to minister and me to write.

Furthermore, I want to thank the editorial staff of InterVarsity Press, particularly Cindy Bunch, for making this an enjoyable process.

And I want to acknowledge my parents, Arthur and Lois, though they are no longer living, for all they did to give me a good foundation in faith and life.

Last but not least, I want to thank Connie, my wife, who encouraged and coaxed me to write and took our boys away for a few weeks so I could have uninterrupted writing time. She has also been a helpful editor, improving my writing and giving energy and life to my words. Thank you, Connie, for all you do.

PART 1

ABSOLUTES
WITHOUT
ABSOLUTISM

WHAT IS TRUTH?

BILL: *Are you one of those Christians who believe in absolute truth?*

JOHN: *Well, I suppose I am. I don't believe that everything is relative.*

BILL: *I think that anybody who holds to absolute truth is oppressive, intolerant, self-righteous, rigid, close-minded and an arrogant know-it-all.*

JOHN: *Wow! I didn't think I was all that. In fact, I would say that the kinds of attitudes and actions you describe are inconsistent with faith in Christ.*

BILL: *You mean to say that a belief in absolutes is not oppressive?*

JOHN: *The Bible, from beginning to end, is opposed to injustice of any kind— look at the prophets and at Jesus' teaching. You need absolutes like those the Bible provides to even say that oppression is objectively or really bad.*

BILL: *But look at the examples of oppression caused by those who held to absolutes: the Inquisition, the Crusades, Islamic fundamentalism and even Marxism and Nazism.*

JOHN: *You're right. Many people who believe in absolutes have become what I call absolutists. But I believe in absolutes without absolutism. Faith in Christ is the opposite of arrogance, intolerance, self-righteousness and the know-it-all, close-minded attitude you described. Let me show you how this is the case.*

⟳

Without using exactly the words exchanged by John and Bill, I have had many such dialogues, not only in the past but also in the process of writing this book. Rarely does a person hear more than one of these negative characteristics mentioned, but just the mention of "truth" or "absolutes" to unbelievers (or even to some believers) is enough to produce blank stares, an uneasy silence or verbal objection. Many people in our society assume that a belief in absolutes can and will lead to abuses. Somewhere down the line, unless we are careful to qualify our terms, our assertion of absolutes will be heard as absolutism.

I am convinced that this need to communicate a rejection of absolutism while continuing to defend absolutes is a new arena for apologetics, one not yet developed. We need to show not only how our beliefs do not necessarily lead to absolutism but also how our faith is necessarily opposed to this oppressive approach. Even more, our faith in Christ provides an antidote (one that relativism lacks) against oppression, arrogance, intolerance, self-righteousness, close-mindedness, defensiveness and other such vices. A healthy knowledge of Christ and his Word is the total cure.

THREE MESSAGES

We must remember that in any communication there are at least three messages: (1) what I intend to say, (2) what I actually say and (3) what others hear. From years of teaching, I know that these three messages can be quite different. At times people have told me that they got something out of my talk that bears little similarity to what I believe I actually said. At other times people have balked at what I had to say, not so much because of its content but because of the manner in which I said it.

This need for care in what message we are sending is especially important when we are speaking about moral absolutes or truth. As I have indicated above, many equate absolute truth with oppression. You may intend to say that there are fixed points by which you can orient yourself in this crazy world and be heard as advocating the Inquisition, the Crusades or something like Nazism. In today's environment it is important to stress those aspects of our beliefs that prevent us from becoming arrogant and oppressive toward others. We need to point out that many biblical teachings, including those of Christ, can serve as a corrective to oppression.

The word *absolutism* is sometimes used by Christian authors as synonymous with a belief in absolutes. I suggest that it is valuable to make a distinction between absolutes and absolutism. Just as a need to *relate* truth to all areas of life does not make us *relativists*, so believing that there are some *moral absolutes* does not make us *absolutists*. Usually the *-ist* or *-ism* in *relativism* or *relativist* indicates a more extreme position. Thus the *-ism* in *absolutism* may indicate an extreme position with respect to absolutes.

Absolutism might be defined as being synonymous with a cluster of characteristics: arrogance, close-mindedness, intolerance, self-righteousness, bigotry and the like. Absolutists are those who think everything is "black and white" and who make few if any allowances for ambiguity or uncertainty. You and I know of some characters, like TV's Archie Bunker, who talk at you, not with you. They act as if they have the answer for everything, and in the process, if they claim to follow Jesus, they drive many would-be seekers away from Christianity.

THE CRISIS OF TRUTH

If we are successful in dismantling the kinds of psychological obstacles mentioned above, we can then move on to a critique of relativism. And we must, for the most important issue for church and culture in the twenty-first century is the issue of truth.

ᏇᎠᏇ

BILL: *All right, you've convinced me that faith in Christ does not necessarily lead to absolutism. But what difference would it make to me if I decided to believe in absolutes? Why does it matter?*

JOHN: *Well, if you don't believe in some absolutes, then you don't have anything solid to believe about meaning, dignity, morality or Christ. It would only be your taste or personal preference.*

BILL: *If I did come to believe in Christ as you do (and I am definitely not there yet), couldn't I believe that Christ is just true for me and not for somebody else?*

JOHN: *Many people do feel that way, to be sure, but that would be radically different from what believers have held through the centuries. If you don't believe that Jesus Christ lives today and that his teachings are decisive, your faith will lack any power to affect your life. It will not be something that will cause you to sacrifice anything you really want, much less be something for which you would be willing to die.*

BILL: *You mean that faith in Christ is a fact?*

JOHN: *Yes, I believe the good news of Christ is a fact—what Francis Schaeffer called "true truth," that is, truth that is true independently of your preference about it. In fact, C. S. Lewis once wrote that Christianity "if true is of infinite importance, but if not true is of no importance. The one thing it cannot be is of moderate importance."*

BILL: *I thought Christianity was just a leap of faith—a leap into the darkness.*

JOHN: *I can't prove to you all the specific things that I believe, but there is sufficient evidence from reason, experience, history and practice to convince me that relativism is false and faith in Christ is true. I would call my faith a leap into the direction set by the light.*

BILL: *Why do you believe relativism is wrong?*

JOHN: *Because relativism is inconsistent in theory and in practice. It goes totally against what we already know.*

᷍᷍᷍

At the foundation of our culture, the ancient question asked by Pilate echoes, "What is truth?" (Jn 18:38). Many in our society are convinced that nothing is absolutely true. Even more, they say nothing is completely right or completely wrong. Truth, morality and justice are all relative to one's individual preferences or those of the group to which one belongs. I have been in meetings where statements like "whose morality?" and "whose justice?" were thought to be the ultimate trump card, and no one could say anything more about absolutes after such a statement was made.

Many segments of our general culture reject the idea of universal or absolute truth. Secular relativists, participants in New Age spirituality and some persons described as postmodern, using argument and accusation, assault those who express certainty about truth. Their objective seems to be a life floating in tempest-tossed seas without any anchor.

This cultural erosion has had a major impact on our spiritual beliefs. For instance, according to surveys the number of people in the United States who profess to believe that God exists, that Christ is the Son of God and that he was raised from the dead is staggeringly high (belief in God is above 90 percent).[1] Yet the same people—or at least a great majority of them—refuse to believe in absolutes.[2] This discrepancy points to a failure of people to make a connection between their belief in God and absolute truth. Many believe the same things people used to believe, but not in the same decisive way.

Within the church we find an erosion of confidence in the nature of truth. About half of those who describe themselves as born again also say they do not believe in absolutes.[3] Among many churchgoing people under thirty years of age (so called Generation X, Y or younger), even the *mention* of truth produces a negative reaction. In my experience of working regularly with committed believers just out of college, these young men and women do not hesitate to call what they believe "true," but only with great difficulty can they call another religious or ethical opinion "false." One such believer who had just graduated from a secular university commented that even the mention of an argument against other views or a giving of reasons for faith brought up in him a powerful negative emotional reaction.

Not only is the concept of truth suspect but so also is the discipline of rational argumentation.[4] And yet, as the great apologist C. S. Lewis held, learning how to counter relativism is essential as a preparation for proclaiming the gospel. He said,

> For my part, I believe that we ought to work not only at spreading the gospel (that certainly) but also at a certain preparation for the gospel. It is necessary to recall many to the Law of Nature before we talk about God. Christ promises forgiveness of sins, but what is that to those who, since they do not know the Law of Nature, do not know that they have sinned? Who will take the medicine unless he knows he is in the grip of disease? Moral relativity is the enemy we have to overcome before we tackle atheism.[5]

If this "preparation" was necessary in Lewis's era (he lived from 1898 to 1963), it is even more important in our time. Relativism and how we address it will profoundly influence our evangelism and discipleship. If we are to see any revival or reformation, we have to challenge relativism as a precondition for proclaiming the gospel and for living out the lordship of Jesus in our lives.

The uncertainty about truth in our society does not bode well for the spread of the gospel as it has been classically believed and lived by Christians through the ages. What was described by C. S. Lewis as "mere Christianity," or by Vincent of Lérins as that which is held "everywhere, always and by all," is being progressively undermined, not so much by direct assault as by *erosion*—erosion of the stark clarity with which truth was formerly stated. We need to make sure that our foundation is solid.

RELATIVISTS OF MANY STRIPES

In the intellectual arena, as is well known, many hold to relativism of one kind or another.[6] Meanwhile, on a popular level, relativism is at work in our culture under various folk religious guises. For example, New Age spirituality is clearly relativistic and presents to us Eastern religious perspectives in Western dress. Another related movement is neopaganism, including varieties of the new witchcraft known as the Craft or Wicca. Neopagans strongly reject the idea of absolute truth. The relativism held by these different movements has different emphases, but at the root there are strong similarities. I will attempt to offer a response to relativism in this book that is applicable to all these groups.

Many good evangelical books have been written in recent years on the topic of truth. I have learned greatly from many of them.[7] In this book I will be attempting to make many complex arguments as clear as I can for the student who wants to understand more about current debates about truth but lacks an understanding of the academic arguments. In some sections this book may cause you to stretch your mind to grasp things that seem difficult to understand. In other sections it may seem to you that I am simplifying too much. It has been my experience that all conceptualization involves oversimplification, and I am particularly aware of it here. My goal is to address intelligent believers without much background in this subject and to bring them to a further understanding of the issues involved as well as to point them to excellent resources that can expand their grasp of the material. If you start with all the complexities, you become incomprehensible. If you start simply and clearly, you can always graduate to more and more complex qualifications.

I am starting with a basic understanding of truth as *that which corresponds to reality, as perceived by God.*[8] Only God sees reality in all its complexity. What we understand is partial and limited. Yet partial truth can be real truth as long as we do not take it for the whole truth. Because we are made in the image of God, we have the capacity to understand what we need to know about creation and about God.

OUTLINE OF THE BOOK

The first half of the book will demonstrate how we can uphold objective truth or morality without being absolutists. As believers in absolutes, we can be—and ought to be—in the forefront as defenders of tolerance, rightly defined (chapter two). Followers of Christ ought to be the last to speak and act in a self-righteous manner because of who Christ is and what he has done for us (chapter three). It is not necessarily arrogant to make assertions of truth; in fact, faith in Christ requires assertions made without arrogance (chapter four). We can afford to admit the ambiguity in much of our knowledge of the world as well as our difficulty in relating truth to complex situations (chapters five and six). And finally it is important that we are able to give a defense without defensiveness (chapter seven).

In the second half of the book we will see why arguments often fail and what strategies to take when they do fail (chapter eight). We will see that relativists are often absolutists in disguise (chapter nine) and that relativism has dire consequences (chapter ten). Relativism is self-contradictory (chapter eleven), leads to the absurd conclusions that everybody is right and nobody is right (chapter twelve) and has no room for evil (chapter thirteen). In other words, relativism is inconsistent theoretically and practically.

Throughout this book I will make frequent references to C. S. Lewis. For fifteen years I have been scholar-in-residence at the C. S. Lewis Institute and have regularly taught courses on C. S. Lewis's life, thought and apologetics. Lewis believed that his most important work was *The Abolition of Man*—a book on relativism. He wrote frequently on this topic, not only in *The Abolition of Man* but also in many other places. Lewis stated his arguments so clearly and powerfully that, during my writing, his emphases often came to my mind.

I have not sought originality or novelty in this book but have desired to help you become more certain of the truth and thus become better able to articulate, defend and live faith in Christ in personal and public life. Truth is the decisive issue of our time, and the ability to communicate absolutes without absolutism is an essential precondition for the gospel (and other truths) to be heard.

In the end it is not my place or your place to convince anyone of the truth. The Holy Spirit can do that without you or me. I can only be a signpost pointing the way down the road. I am simply asking you to listen to the biblical passages presented and the arguments given, and see if you can gain a clearer vision for your life and discipleship.

Millions of people on this planet are out of alignment with what is good, true, right and real. This alignment needs to start with finding the foundation by which all truths must be judged—the true truth, which is found in Jesus Christ's life, work and teachings. This truth must never be watered down, never be compromised and never be forgotten, lest our world fall into an abyss of unreality. This book's goal is to encourage disciples of Jesus Christ to tear down any obstacle to the knowledge of God and take every thought captive to Christ (2 Cor 10:3-5).

True Tolerance

BILL: *I think a Christian assertion of absolute truth leads to intolerance.*

JOHN: *I certainly agree that there have been many intolerant Christians throughout the ages and that intolerance is wrong. But do you think that intolerance is wrong and tolerance is right?*

BILL: *Of course.*

JOHN: *Don't you realize that you've just made an objective moral judgment? You've said something is really right and something is really wrong. I thought you believed everything was relative?*

BILL: *Don't try to trap me. I'm just saying that Christianity is intolerant.*

JOHN: *Believers in Christ have a solid foundation for defending tolerance— a foundation that relativism lacks, by the way. In fact, I call cultural relativistic tolerance "false tolerance." Tolerance has become the relativists' only "absolute."*

BILL: *Why is it false?*

JOHN: *Because it provides no basis for tolerance to be right. A believer, on the other hand, can call tolerance really right and intolerance really wrong.*

BILL: *Doesn't tolerance lead to the idea that all views are equal? I didn't think you held to that.*

JOHN: *No, I don't. But believers can argue for legal and social tolerance without obliterating deep differences. I think that relativistic tolerance, on the other hand, pretends to embrace everyone while actually being exclusive.*

BILL: *I don't get it. Explain what you mean.*

JOHN: *Okay. Let me show you how a believer can uphold tolerance and a relativist can't.*

⟨⟨∞⟩⟩

Mark is a medical student who happened to mention in class that he is a believer in Christ. Not long after, his adviser called him in and said, "I'm concerned, given your religious views, about whether or not you can be a good doctor. By that I mean whether or not you'll be able to be tolerant of your patients' various religious beliefs. It could affect how you function on a hospital staff with other doctors and nurses too."

Ann is a graduate student in counseling at a secular institution. She has been told that in the name of tolerance she must help students work through, accept and embrace sexual practices and lifestyles that she, as a Christian believer, regards as wrong.

Michelle began to wonder why she was not being considered for partner at her law firm even though for years she had brought in as much business and had handled as many important cases as anyone in the firm. Then one day one of the secretaries confided to her, "I heard two of the partners talking. They were agreeing that, because you're 'one of those born-again Christians,' you're going to turn out to be too 'black and white' on business issues. So they're not comfortable offering you partnership."

Often those who believe in objective truth are thought of as intolerant, merely because we believe that something is good or evil, true or false. Is this fair? Is it reasonable?

Tolerance (in the relativist sense) has no reason for being thought of as the "right" position. In fact, in this sense tolerance is not really right and intolerance is not really wrong. In many ways it is a "false tolerance." It is false because it implicitly undermines the basis and motive for tolerance.

On the other hand, believers have many solid reasons for being defenders of tolerance, and we have a sure foundation for upholding this virtue.

It is time we learned how to make a stand for the distinction between true tolerance and false tolerance. It is time for believers to regain the moral high ground on the issue of tolerance.

TOLERANCE IS A VIRTUE AND INTOLERANCE A VICE

In the secular version of tolerance, there are no absolutes and everything is relative. That means that tolerance is not really objectively good and intolerance is not really objectively evil. There is no basis other than personal preference to uphold tolerance and condemn intolerance. In some quarters tolerance seems to be the only "absolute," but of course there are no absolute values or virtues, not even tolerance.

On the other hand, true tolerance is the kind that can and ought to be defended by believers because we have good reasons for maintaining that rightly defined tolerance is a virtue and rightly defined intolerance is a vice. For the believer there is an adequate basis to sustain this virtue and teach it to our children.

The virtue of tolerance extends to include a legal tolerance for diverse religious practices as well as social tolerance for people who are different from ourselves.

LEGAL TOLERANCE

We, as U.S. Christians, have a good basis for being defenders of religious liberty and the First Amendment.

First, many of the initial settlers in this country left England because their religious liberty was being threatened. You could call religious liberty and tolerance America's first freedom.

Second, we do not believe that one can or ought to physically coerce someone else into religious belief, such as occurred during the Inquisition or during the persecution of the Scottish Covenanters. We can defend people's legal rights even when we believe them to be wrong from our perspective, for Scripture defends the right to freedom of conscience (see Rom 14:23).

Third, we have a good reason for desiring the nonestablishment of a particular religion or denomination. Generally, where religion has been established, it has become diluted and weak; where it has been allowed freedom, it has thrived. Look at the dwindling established churches (with a few exceptions) in England, Scandinavia and Europe, and contrast this situation with the vitality (despite many imperfections) of nonestablished Christianity in America. At the founding of this country, only about 10 percent of people attended church once a week. At present, about 40 percent attend church in a given week. This demonstrates that where there is full freedom to persuade, the most attractive options gain the most adherents.

Finally, the best way to retain our own freedoms is to be defenders of others' freedom. Do we want justice or "just us"?[1] Missiologist Lesslie Newbigin said,

> If we acknowledge the God of the Bible, we are committed to struggle for justice in society, justice means giving to each his due. Our problem (as seen in light of the Gospel) is that each of us overestimates what is due to him as compared with what is due to his neighbor. . . . If I do not acknowledge a justice which judges the justice for which I fight, I am an agent, not of justice, but of lawless tyranny.[2]

SOCIAL TOLERANCE

Christ encourages in us a broader love, encompassing not only family, friends and neighbors but even our enemies. Christ's radical call to "love our enemies" is unique among the world religions. He extends the love of neighbor to the love of enemies.

In Jesus' day a debate raged as to who was included in the definition of "neighbor," and some sought to draw Jesus into the debate. On one occasion a lawyer asked Christ, "Who is my neighbor?" (Lk 10:29). New Testament scholar T. W. Manson commented that even the question is revealing: "The question is unanswerable and ought not to be asked. For love does not begin by defining its objects; it discovers them."[3] Jesus' parable of the Good Samaritan establishes his view on being a neighbor to others.

Meanwhile, some other Jewish leaders insisted that Gentiles, heretics or Samaritans were not neighbors. A rabbinic comment, or "midrash," on Ruth says that Jews should not seek the death of Gentiles, "but if they be in any danger of death, we are not bound to deliver them; e.g. if any of them fall into the sea, you *shall not need* to take them out for it is said, 'Thou shalt not rise up against the blood of thy neighbor', but such a one is not your neighbor."[4]

In the Jewish apocryphal book Sirach we see similar advice given.

> If you do a kindness, know to whom you do it,
> and you will be thanked for your good deeds.
> Do good to a godly man, and you will be repaid—
> if not by him, certainly by the Most High. . . .
> Give to the godly man, but do not help the sinner.
> Do good to the humble, but do not give to the ungodly;
> hold back his bread, and do not give it to him,
> lest by means of it he subdue you;
> for you will receive twice as much evil
> for all the good which you do to him.
> For the Most High also hates sinners
> and will inflict punishment on the ungodly.
> Give to the good man, but do not help the sinner. (Sir 12:1-7 RSV)

In contrast to other teachings of the time, Jesus' story of the Good Samaritan casts as an unlikely hero a class of persons who were often hated because of theological and historical rivalry. To orthodox Jews, Samaritans were more despised than Gentiles. Jesus not only made a Samaritan the hero but he also implicitly identified himself with this one so despised.

We may ask, "Who are the Samaritans today?" Who are those whom we have a difficult time loving? Who are those toward whom we feel no compassion? They are those people whom Christ calls us to love. We are called to love across deep religious, cultural, ethnic and racial divisions. The picture shown to us in heaven is of an assembly made up of every tribe, tongue, people and nation (see Rev 5:9). Christ is such a great leader that he can command respect and love from the most diverse crowd of followers. Believers should be on the forefront of upholding a multicultural vision, embracing with love people from every culture. There is no basis for ethnocentrism here; Jesus is not Western or Eastern, and his church knows no cultural boundaries.[5]

Even in the case of people who are not just different but religiously and morally objectionable, we are to love. The apostle Paul reaffirmed Jesus' teaching in Romans 12:14-21:

> Bless those who persecute you; bless and do not curse. . . . Never pay back evil for evil to anyone. . . . Never take your own revenge, beloved, but leave room for the wrath of God, for it is written, "Vengeance is Mine, I will repay," says the Lord. But if your enemy is hungry, feed him, and if he is thirsty, give him a drink; for in so doing you will heap burning coals on his head. Do not be overcome by evil, but overcome evil with good.

Jesus' call to love our enemies takes us beyond a passive tolerance to a proactive love that needs to be demonstrated across religious, ethnic, cultural, racial and moral divides. No matter how broad the chasm, Christ's love extends there. Love is both centripetal and centrifugal: it both attracts people toward those who love and thrusts us out to love people wherever they live and whatever their stance.[6]

NOT MORAL EQUIVALENCE

Tolerance does not imply religious and moral equivalence. It is in the making of this distinction that false tolerance and true tolerance diverge.

Some cultural forms of tolerance minimize the differences among views. If your religion is merely true for you and my religion true for me, then what we believe is a matter of arbitrary personal preference. Truth is not at issue here.

The reasons for such a position may be many. Certainly one reason is that some fear that a rigorous debate about truth will lead to violence. And this has, in fact, been the case at times. But is it possible to conduct a debate in a vigorous but civil matter? Of course. G. K. Chesterton (1874–1936) once said, "The problem with a quarrel is that it spoils a good argument."

The issue of truth has become inconvenient and potentially dangerous, and so it has been shoved aside or defined away by saying it is true that there are no truths. Consider the following illustration by Francis Beckwith.

Teacher: "Welcome students. Since this is the first day of class, I want to lay down some ground rules. First, since no one has the truth, you should be open-minded to the opinions of your fellow students. Second . . . Elizabeth, do you have a question?"

Elizabeth: "Yes, I do. If nobody has the truth, isn't that the reason for me not to listen to my fellow students? After all, if nobody has the truth, why should I waste my time listening to other people and their opinions? What would be the point? Only if somebody has the truth does it make sense to be open-minded. Don't you agree?"

Teacher: "No, I don't. Are you claiming to know the truth? Isn't that a bit arrogant and dogmatic?"

Elizabeth: "Not at all. Rather, I think it is dogmatic as well as arrogant to assert that there is not one person on earth that knows the truth. After all, have you met every person in the world and quizzed him or her exhaustively? If not, how can you make such a claim? Also, I believe it is actually the opposite of arrogance to say that I will alter my opinions to fit the truth whenever and wherever I find it. And I happen to think that I have good reason to believe I do know the truth and would like to share it with you. Why won't you listen to me? Why would you automatically discredit my opinion before it is even uttered? I thought we were supposed to listen to everyone's opinions."

Teacher: "This should prove to be an interesting semester."

Another student: (blurts out) "Ain't that the truth." (The students laugh.)[7]

As this dialogue suggests, holding to eternal truth does not necessarily make you arrogant. In fact, if I have carefully weighed Christ's claims and find that the mass of evidence points to his being the way, the truth and the life, and if I have come to acknowledge that he is the Lord, then it would be arrogant for me to reject what my Lord says. If I were to say that Christ is the way because he is *my* way, that would be arrogant. But if I have submitted myself to his claims, then I could humbly put forward what I have discovered. This is not to say that arrogant presentations of Christ are uncommon, only that arrogance is discouraged by such a discovery. Francis Schaeffer (1912–1984) once argued that Christianity is the easiest and the hardest of religions. It is the easiest in that all you have to do is say, "God, be merciful to me, the sinner!" (Lk 18:13). It is the hardest because humbling your pride is the very hardest thing to do. We have two choices: to be humble now or be humbled later. An arrogant Christian ought to be an oxymoron. Faith in Christ should be an antidote to arrogance rather than a cause of it.

True tolerance is needed only if differences are significant. As we have seen, true tolerance presupposes deep differences among views. Tolerance is not needed if someone's views are the same or virtually the same or insignificant. The kind of tolerance that minimizes differences makes tolerance unnecessary.

TOLERANCE AS SLOTH

Dorothy Sayers (1893–1957) saw the danger of a false understanding of tolerance in her day. In "The Pantheon Papers" she has a humorous note on "St. Luke of Laodicea, Martyr" (see Rev 3:16):

> St. Lukewarm was a magistrate in the city of Laodicea under Claudius (Emp. A.D. 41-54). He was so broadminded as to offer asylum and patronage to every kind of religious cult, however unorthodox and repulsive, saying in answer to all remonstrance: There is always some truth in everything. This liberality earned for him the surname of "The Tolerator."[8]

Later he fell into the hands of one of the groups he tolerated and was eaten, but his flesh was so tough and tasteless that he was spit out.

In another essay, "The Other Six Deadly Sins," Sayers equated sloth and tolerance:

> The Church names the sixth Deadly Sin Acedia or Sloth. In the world it calls itself Tolerance; but in Hell it is called Despair. It is the accomplice of the other sins and their worst punishment. It is the sin that believes in nothing, cares for nothing, seeks to know nothing, interferes with nothing, enjoys nothing, loves nothing, hates nothing, finds purpose in nothing, lives for nothing, and only remains alive because there is nothing it would die for. We have known it far too well for many years.[9]

All inclusivists sooner or later become exclusivists. Inclusivists are persons who want to draw their circle so that everyone is tolerantly included. They want to embrace everyone, yet the first group of people they exclude are the exclusivists. The inclusivists tend to accept only those who are willing to come under their umbrella or accept their terms of surrender. Appearing to give you a loving embrace, they give you a fatal hug. Have you ever had someone sneak up behind you, put his arms around you, pick you up and squeeze you so that it felt like your ribs would break? Inclusivists want to do even more: you are squeezed until you die to your own individual or corporate assertion of truth. You are accepted only if you are assimilated by them. I think of the Borg on the television series *Star Trek: The Next Generation*, whose refrain was "You will be assimilated. Resistance is futile." As long as you are willing to be drawn inside the inclusivists' circle (assimilated into the collective), you are included. But if you choose to remain outside, asserting your individual beliefs, you are rejected.

Os Guinness talked about an instance of Buddhists complaining that Hindus wanted to "strangle them by the fraternal embrace."[10] False tolerance embraces but strangles any exclusive claim to truth. Another analogy might be drawn from the movie series *The Godfather*. When the godfather kissed a person on the lips, it might have appeared to an unknowledgeable bystander to have been an act of affection; however, those who knew what it meant called it the "kiss of death."[11] On the surface, inclusivism appears loving and embracing, but in reality it kills any exclusive individual or corporate claim to truth.

Relativism is Western and ethnocentric. This demand for assimilation or absorption also applies culturally. Once I was giving a talk at a liberal seminary on Eastern religion. A staff member there accused me of being "Western and ethnocentric" because I dared to critique Eastern religious philosophy. I cannot claim that I responded so clearly then, but I would now respond, "I think that the pluralism and inclusivism put forward at this seminary are Western and ethnocentric."

You can effectively argue that the inclusivism held by many in this culture has clearly Western roots. Many in the Western liberal theological tradition see all religions as basically the same. How could you prove that this is the case? Even more, it seems to be the imposition of Western pluralism on other cultures' religious views. Alister McGrath argued particularly in reference to the pluralism of theologian John Hick, but his point can apply to others as well:

Yet is not this approach shockingly imperialist? Hicks' implication is that it is not; it is only the educated Western liberal academic who can understand all the religions. Their adherents may believe that they have access to the truth; in fact, only the Western liberal academic has such privileged access, which is denied to those who belong to and practice such a religion.[12]

Later, McGrath commented,

The belief that all religions are ultimately expressions of the same transcendent reality is at best illusory and at worst oppressive—illusory because it lacks any substantiating basis and oppressive because it involves the systematic imposition of the agenda of those in positions of intellectual power on the religions and those who adhere to them. The illiberal imposition of this pluralistic metanarrative on religions is ultimately a claim to mastery—both in the sense of having a Nietzschean authority and power to mold material according to one's own will, and in the sense of being able to relativize all the religions by having access to a privileged standpoint.[13]

So this liberal theological inclusivism has clearly Western roots and precedent. And its adherents are also arrogantly, imperialistically imposing their understanding of religion on all the world's religions, whether they want it or not. It is not only Western but ethnocentric because it does not allow the unique truth claims of different world religions to be heard and acknowledged. It does not take seriously the truth claims of world religions.

This same kind of critique could be made of postmodernism. The imposition of the postmodern metanarrative on the world religions is not only Western but also ethnocentric. We can see by its philosophical roots in people like Karl Marx, Friedrich Nietzsche, Ludwig Wittgenstein, Sigmund Freud, Jacques Derrida, Richard Rorty, Stanley Fish, Michel Foucault and others that it is Western. That postmodernism is ethnocentric despite claiming to be multicultural can be shown by its denial that any culture's religious views can be "true truth" for us. To the Chinese, post-modernists might say, "Your views are true for you, given your cultural setting and context, but they have no universal applicability to us." In other words, the Chinese cannot teach us truth where we are in error, nor can we show them errors where we have the truth. That is ethnocentric, an imposition of a Western cultural postmodern mindset that smashes any other culture's claim to universal, eternal truth.

Postmodernism is an oppressive imposition of Western ethnocentrism on the world religions. They are strangled by the "fraternal embrace" and have received the "kiss of death." They have been given the fatal hug.

TRUE TOLERANCE

We have the grounds to defend the virtue of tolerance and condemn the vice of intolerance. We can defend legal tolerance and have a strong mandate for social tolerance. We can be strong defenders of tolerance without holding to religious or moral equivalence. In fact, it is only by maintaining objective moral values that advocating tolerance and opposing intolerance makes moral sense.

RIGHT, NOT RIGHTEOUS

BILL: *All right, you turned the tables on me on the issue of tolerance. But surely you won't deny that many Christians act in a self-righteous manner.*

JOHN: *Sadly, you are right. However, the last people who should act self-righteously are believers. Yet it's a great temptation.*

BILL: *So you are admitting the tendency to self-righteousness?*

JOHN: *Not a necessary tendency but an inevitable temptation. The more you fight against what you believe is wrong and uphold the right, the easier it is to confuse being right with being righteous.*

BILL: *So self-righteousness is almost inevitable for Christians?*

JOHN: *It is not inevitable to fall into self-righteousness, but unless you focus on what Christ and the rest of the Scriptures say, it's easy to succumb to it. Let me point out that many relativists seem self-righteous too.*

BILL: *There you go, trying to turn the tables on me again!*

JOHN: *Sorry, I couldn't resist. Let me emphasize that everything about faith in Christ undermines self-righteousness. It goes directly against the gospel.*

BILL: *How?*

JOHN: *Sometimes Christians wrongly give the impression that they are the righteous people and those outside the church are unrighteous. In fact, those in the church are unrighteous too. That's why there is a need to repent and believe in Jesus.*

BILL: *It seems like many Christians don't understand their own faith.*

JOHN: *You are right. They might have understood it once, but they often forget it.*

ᏻᎳᏳ

The charge has often been made against Christian believers that we seem self-righteous. Sadly, for some this is often the case.

It is important to note that the problem does not lie with the certainty of being right. The problem lies here: Sometimes, when we are waxing eloquent about some injustice, we can begin to feel self-righteous, or at least to give the impression of self-righteousness. And the last people who ought to act or feel self-righteous are those of us who believe in the gospel of Christ. Right does not mean righteous.

LOOK TO YOURSELVES

Jesus used the quotation "Do not judge so that you will not be judged" (Mt 7:1) to condemn judgmentalism. He went on to say:

> For in the way you judge, you will be judged; and by your standard of measure, it will be measured to you. Why do you look at the speck that is in your brother's eye, but do not notice the log that is in your own eye? Or how can you say to your brother, "Let me take the speck out of your eye," and behold, the log is in your own eye? You hypocrite, first take the log out of your own eye, and then you will see clearly to take the speck out of your brother's eye. (Mt 7:1-5)

Certainly, Jesus desires us to look to ourselves first before we criticize others. But does this mean that we have to be *perfect* to make judgments, that is, to make critical distinctions between right and wrong, truth and error? No. In the next verse Jesus said, "Do not give what is holy to dogs, and do not throw your pearls before swine, or they will trample them under their feet, and turn and tear you to pieces" (Mt 7:6). We are expected to discern even though we are not perfect.

In Galatians we see a similar call in the context of exposing another's sin: look to yourself. Paul wrote:

> Brethren, even if anyone is caught in any trespass, you who are spiritual, restore such a one in a spirit of gentleness; *each one looking to yourself, so that you too will not be tempted.* Bear one another's burdens, and thereby fulfill the law of Christ. For if anyone thinks he is something when he is nothing, he deceives himself. (Gal 6:1-3, emphasis added)

Note that this matter of criticizing another is for the "spiritual," and it is to be done in a "spirit of gentleness," always "looking to yourself." A great problem, the text goes on to say, is overestimating our own importance—and consequently underestimating another's importance. It is self-deceit to think that you are "something" when you are "nothing."

Even in the case where church discipline is exercised (see 1 Cor 5:1-7), we are warned: "You should rather forgive and comfort him, otherwise such a one might be overwhelmed by excessive sorrow. Wherefore I urge you to reaffirm your love for him" (2 Cor 2:7-8). This certainly does not encourage a self-righteous, judgmental spirit.

RIGHT, NOT RIGHTEOUS

As we read in Luke 13:1-5, some people told Jesus the story of an atrocity committed by Pontius Pilate, governor of Judea.

> Now on the same occasion there were some present who reported to Him [Jesus] about the Galileans whose blood Pilate had mixed with their sacrifices. And Jesus said to them, "Do you suppose that these Galileans were greater sinners than all other Galileans because they suffered this fate? I tell you, no, but unless you repent, you will all likewise perish. Or do you suppose that those eighteen on whom the tower in Siloam fell and killed them were worse culprits than all the men who live in Jerusalem? I tell you no, but unless you repent, you will all likewise perish."

In the first story we see a great atrocity, combining murder and sacrilege. The Galileans were killed while they were offering sacrifices. It would be as if terrorists came into a church and shot worshipers as they were partaking of Communion, then mingled their blood with the Communion wine. Imagine if such a story were told to you. How would you respond? "That's awful! Who could be capable of committing such a horrendous crime?" Can you imagine responding, "You know, you're not that righteous yourself"? Imagine that kind of response to the story of a Middle Eastern atrocity committed in our day. Amazingly, a warning against spiritual overconfidence was Jesus' line of response.

First, Jesus said, "Do you suppose that these Galileans were greater sinners?" (Lk 13:2). He directly contradicted the misunderstanding that there is always a one-to-one relationship between sin and suffering. We can see this same fallacy at work in the heads of Job's "comforters." For instance, Eliphaz said to Job, "Who ever perished being innocent?" (Job 4:7). And when Jesus' disciples came to him and asked about a man born blind, they said, "Who sinned, this man or his parents?" Jesus responded, "It was neither that this man sinned, nor his parents; but it was so that the works of God might be displayed in him" (Jn 9:2-3). Jesus said something similar regarding the Galilean tragedy: it was a fallacy to assume that these Galileans were greater sinners than others.

The second part of his response, however, is a shocker. Perhaps Jesus suspected a political trap, tempting him to make a traitorous remark about Pilate that could later be used against him. Perhaps he discerned self-righteousness in those who reported the atrocity. Perhaps they felt that, because they were so clearly on the side of the right, they were righteous. Jesus was quick to indicate otherwise. "I tell you, no, but unless you repent, you will all likewise perish" (Lk 13:5). It is surprising that Jesus was not killed on the spot.

In the second story Jesus mentioned another tragedy in which a tower in Siloam fell and killed eighteen people. This might be considered an "act of God." It also might have political overtones. Alfred Edersheim speculated that the eighteen killed in this story were working on Pilate's aqueduct. It is known that Pilate took money from the temple treasury and used it to build an aqueduct. This then would combine tragedy with political corruption and sacrilege. Perhaps people thought those working on such a dubious project deserved the judgment of God. Jesus again told them that unless they repented, they would likewise perish.

It is easy to move from the assertion that our cause is just to the erroneous conclusion that we are just (righteous) people. Kenneth Bailey said about this passage:

> Those who suffer political oppression often quickly assume that their suffering is the only kind that matters, and a crass indifference may then develop to the suffering of others around them, particularly if it is of a nonpolitical nature. . . . Those who fight for a just cause often assume that the struggle makes them righteous. It does not. The more intense the struggle for justice, the more the oppressed tend to assume their own righteousness. This assumption of righteousness at times expresses itself as an arrogance that refuses any criticism. . . . Furthermore, after all that we have suffered, how dare you inflict more wounds on us by your criticism?[1]

It is easy for those who struggle for social justice on a national or international level to encounter this temptation to self-righteousness. It is especially easy in political debates to demonize the other side. The attitude is all too common: we are the angels; they are the devils. Again, Bailey (who lived for many years in the Middle East) said, "Evil forces are at work in your movement that will destroy you. . . . You must repent or all of you will be destroyed by these forces. . . . Blessed is the movement that is willing to listen to a courageous voice quietly insisting, 'There are devils among us and angels among them. We must repent.' "[2]

Despite the absence of a basis for real justice and righteousness in their views, you can see this self-righteous attitude in postmodernists,

New Agers and neopagans as they rage against the oppression caused by those who believe in absolutes. One theologian spoke for many when he objected to religious intolerance: "The God of monotheism, meaning one God and one truth, ought to be dead."[3] Many rage against the Inquisition, the Crusades and missionary abuses past and present. You can hear in this the note "We are the angels and they are the devils." Self-righteousness has crept in unawares.

While recognizing these faulty claims and attitudes in others, it is critically important that we examine our own hearts, our own words and our own actions. How much have we in the church been guilty of a self-righteous attitude? I would say it is inevitable that we will feel and occasionally succumb to this temptation. The more we are fighting the "culture wars" or social injustice, the greater the tendency is to move from "we are right" to "we are righteous." We must repent. Bailey summarized, "Any intense political movement must look deep within its own soul to repent of its own evil, lest it destroy itself and the very people it seeks to serve."[4]

To enter the kingdom of God, we must repent and believe. But to reiterate an earlier point, repentance does not stop there. Martin Luther's number-one thesis, posted on the Wittenberg church door on October 31, 1517, was this: "That the entire life of the faithful should be repentance." Luther (1483–1546) and John Calvin (1509–1564) wanted to do away with the abuses of the confessional, but not the practice of confessing sins itself. A perfunctory prayer of confession during worship is not enough. Some of the early Puritans kept daily diaries of their sins so that they would regularly repent and confess their sins. Their diaries were their confessionals. One of them, William Fenner, said, "Better to sleep in a house full of adders and venomous serpents than to sleep in one sin."[5]

One of the weaknesses of the evangelical church is that it offers little place for repentance. Acknowledging one's sin is seen as too negative. However, unless we repent regularly, we deprive ourselves of the joys of forgiveness and the pardon received as a result. Moreover, we leave ourselves vulnerable to a holier-than-thou attitude. The less our emphasis on repentance, the greater our tendency to self-righteousness.

Even more, the gospel of Christ calls us to put our trust in Christ's righteousness, not in our own.

NOT RIGHTEOUS IN OURSELVES

Jesus told the parable of the Pharisee and the tax collector to those who "trusted in themselves that they were righteous, and viewed others with contempt" (Lk 18:9). By means of this story, he exposed self-justification for what it is—ugly and self-defeating.

> Two men went up into the temple to pray, one a Pharisee and the other a tax collector. The Pharisee stood and was praying this to himself, "God, I thank You that I am not like other people: swindlers, unjust, adulterers, or even like this tax collector. I fast twice a week; I pay tithes of all that I get." But the tax collector, standing some distance away, was even unwilling to lift up his eyes to heaven, but was beating his breast, saying, "God, be merciful to me, the sinner!" I tell you, this man went to his house justified rather than the other; for everyone who exalts himself will be humbled, but he who humbles himself will be exalted. (Lk 18:10-14)

The two men—the Pharisee and the tax collector—went up to the temple to pray. It is reasonable to assume that they were "going up" for the morning or evening sacrifice. The morning sacrifice was offered regularly at dawn, and the evening sacrifice at three o'clock in the afternoon. The lamb was offered in sacrifice, followed by public and private prayer. The Pharisee prayed "to himself," during an opportunity for private prayer, thanking God that he was not like tax collectors, who were notorious for being "swindlers" and "unjust." He also threw in adultery for good measure. He then went on to show why he was holier than others: he fasted more than required—twice a week, in fact. The Old Testament law required fasting only on the Day of Atonement (see Lev 23:29). More than that, the Pharisee tithed on everything he got, rather than just tithing on grain, wine and oil, as mandated (Lev 27:30). He did *more* than the Law required and was proud of it.

It is of interest to note that the phrase "stood and was praying this to himself" (Lk 18:11) might also be translated "stood by himself praying." If this were the case, then it would underline the standoffish attitude of this Pharisee. He did not want to come close to the people of the land, because contact with them was thought to produce ritual defilement. That this holier-than-thou attitude was sometimes present among observant Jews is testified to indirectly by the great rabbinic teacher Hillel (a contemporary of Jesus), who said: "Keep not aloof from the congregation and trust not in thyself until the day of thy death, and judge not thy fellow until thou are thyself come to his place."[6] This attitude was being condemned in that time by some leaders of Judaism.

The tax collector, it seems, understood the cultural conventions enough to "stand some distance away" (Lk 18:13). He could only look down, perhaps in contrast with the Pharisee's looking up to heaven. The tax collector also "beat his breast." This was an unusual sign of humility, sorrow and grief. "Beating the breast" appears only twice in the entire Bible, here and in Luke 23:48. According to the latter verse, after Christ's death, the crowds who had observed "this spectacle" went away "beating their breasts." It was especially unusual for men to "beat their breast." This action underlines the tax collector's sorrow for his sin.

The tax collector also said, "God, be merciful to me, the sinner!" (Lk 18:13). The word translated "merciful to me" is, in the Greek, *hiastheti moi*. The root from which this word comes, *hilaskomai*, is the word used for "atonement," "sacrifice" or "propitiation." Another translation indicated in the margin of some Bibles is "God, be propitious to me, a sinner," or "Make atonement for me, a sinner." The tax collector pleaded that the atonement sacrifice for sin offered before God's eyes be effective (propitious) to deal with his sin.

His prayer was granted, the Bible tells us. He "went to his house justified rather than the other" (Lk 18:14). Two had "gone up" to the temple to pray. Both went down, but only one was "justified." The word used here, *dikaioo*, is a root word for justification. Joachim Jeremias thus said, "Our passage shows . . . that the Pauline doctrine of justification has its roots in Jesus' teaching."[7]

Righteousness comes not by trusting in our own righteousness but through looking outside of us to an objective atonement. Those who trust in this "alien" righteousness are justified. Those who trust in their own works are not justified. The unrighteous are forgiven when they humbly plead for atonement. The self-righteous are not forgiven for their sin because they trust in themselves, not in the atoning sacrifice.

Jesus went on to say, "Everyone who exalts himself will be humbled, but he who humbles himself will be exalted" (Lk 18:14). Pride is often considered the mother of the vices. The great North African bishop Augustine (354–430) once said that the most important thing in the spiritual life is humility; in second place, humility; in third place, humility. Pride is an anti-God attitude. It is a spiritual cancer that eats a person from the inside out. Pride that causes someone to look down on others keeps that person from seeing God or others rightly. One cannot look down on others and at the same time look up to our Lord.

John Calvin started out his *Institutes* with the famous words "Nearly all the wisdom we possess, and that is to say, true and sound wisdom, consists of two parts, knowledge of God and of ourselves. . . . It is certain that a man never achieves a clear knowledge of himself unless he has first looked upon God's face and then descends from contemplating Him to scrutinizing himself." Only to the degree that we know God can we come to an accurate knowledge of self. The more we know God, the more we are aware of our finitude and fallenness as well as our dignity— made in the image of God and having our identity in Christ.

We get rid of self-righteousness, not by pointing the finger at others, but by looking at ourselves and repenting of our own sin. Far from trusting in ourselves and in our own goodness, we realize that we must receive our righteousness from Christ's atonement on the cross.

Even when (especially when) we stand on the side of justice, we have to remind ourselves that we are not righteous in ourselves. Even when we grow in Christ, there is wood, hay and stubble mixed in with gold, silver and precious stones (1 Cor 3:12). Whatever fruit we bear, we need to say that it has been God at work in us "to will and to work for His good pleasure" (Phil 2:13). Jesus said, "Apart from me you can do nothing" (Jn 15:5). When we make any progress in our spiritual lives, we have God to thank.

This is not to encourage passivity. I had a professor who used to say that only God could invent a religion where we are called to present 100 percent of our effort to work, pray, study, rebuke, exhort, admonish—yet in the end, what have we contributed to our spiritual growth? Nothing.

Zechariah 4:6 says, " 'Not by might nor by power, but by my Spirit,' says the LORD of hosts." When we make progress, whom do we thank? Ourselves? No! Our Lord? Yes! This ought to keep us humble.

BEFORE THE WATCHING WORLD

As we engage others in the public arena, we need to remember that we are far from perfectly righteous. Whatever advances we have made in the spiritual life are not, strictly speaking, due to ourselves. The only basis on which we are acceptable to God is the righteousness of another who has atoned for our sins—Christ. This leaves no basis for a holier-than-thou attitude. Yet the temptation to this attitude is so great that it needs to be fought against continually. It is easy to say, "Thank God that I am not like that Pharisee."

May we remain vigilant against this attitude in our hearts, in our words and in our actions.

ASSERTIONS
WITHOUT ARROGANCE

BILL: *You have tried to show me that if Christians take their faith seriously they will not be intolerant or self-righteous. Yet it seems to me that just making the kinds of bold assertions I hear Christians make is arrogant.*

JOHN: *Is making any bold assertion arrogant? What about mathematics or the law of gravity or the second law of thermodynamics?*

BILL: *Well, those are facts, so that's different.*

JOHN: *Believers maintain that Christ's life, death and resurrection are facts based on historical evidence similar to those that establish the laws of science, except that past actions are not repeatable.*

BILL: *The Christian claim to exclusive truth seems arrogant.*

JOHN: *If you had been persuaded, like me, by the evidence that Christ is your Lord, then whatever his view of truth, you would need to follow it. In fact, if I call Christ my Lord, then to deliberately deny his view of truth would be an arrogant act of rebellion against him.*

BILL: *Claiming absolutes still seems arrogant to me.*

JOHN: *Believers have held that pride is the mother of the vices. Everything about faith in Christ discourages arrogance.*

Is it possible to make assertions about truth, justice, politics or theology without being arrogant? It is often assumed that any assertion of a belief in religious or moral absolutes implies arrogance. As we will see, the absolute denial of absolutes is arrogant. Relativism arrogantly maintains that there are absolutely no absolutes. On the other hand, absolutes can be asserted without arrogance. Certainly arrogant presentations of Christianity are far too common. But if we have sifted through the evidence, carefully weighed Christ's claims and come to the conclusion that the evidence points to Christ being Lord and Savior, it would be arrogant not to submit to him and share that message with others if he asked us to do so. And in fact, he does just that in Matthew 28:18-20.

An arrogant faith in Christ is a contradiction in terms. Faith in Christ fosters humility rather than arrogance. It is possible to strongly assert the gospel without being arrogant.

THE TIGHTROPE

Once again, if we discover truth, it is not necessarily arrogant to admit it. If we have discovered that $2 + 2 = 4$, that gravity is a force attracting celestial bodies to each other or that the second law of thermodynamics describes the increase of disorder, it is not necessarily arrogant to say so. Some may think that their knowledge of these and other such truths makes them better than others and thus become arrogant. However, the antidote to this arrogance should not involve denying these things to be true. We need to affirm truth but remain humble in the way we hold to it. In almost all cases the truths that we believe are ones we have received from others. Denial of truth leads to blindness about others, about ourselves or about the world around us. Receiving truth when we do find it is humility. Pride or arrogance, on the other hand, involves thinking that we are better, wiser or more knowledgeable than we are in fact. It is to have a false estimation of our capabilities or status.

Paul said in Romans 12:3, "Through the grace given to me I say to everyone among you not to think more highly of himself than he ought to think; but to think so as to have sound judgment, as God has allotted to each a measure of faith." Notice that we are not to think more highly of ourselves than we ought. Neither are we called to think of ourselves as less than we are but instead are to have "sound judgment," or in the Phillips translation, "a sober estimate of our capabilities." Certainly it is easy to be arrogant, thinking more of ourselves than is appropriate. We can see plenty of examples of this tendency. It is just as easy, however, to think less of ourselves than is appropriate, failing to value the gifts, insights and opportunities we have been given.

While we do need to continually look to ourselves (repenting of our sin), we need to beware of doing this too long without also acknowledging who we are in God's sight. We are made in the image of God and we are now accepted "in the Beloved" (Eph 1:6). For instance, although the apostle Paul was deeply aware of the sin in his past and current life, he never dwelt long on his sin without reminding himself of God's grace. In 1 Corinthians 15:9-10 he seems to have been walking a tightrope, balancing to keep from falling off on either side: "I am the least of the apostles, and not fit to be called an apostle, because I persecuted the church of God. But by the grace of God I am what I am, and His grace toward me did not prove vain; but I labored even more than all of them, yet not I, but the grace of God with me." In verse 9 Paul lamented his sin, particularly the persecution of the church (see Acts 7:54—8:3; 9:1-19). Because of this past life, he called himself the "least of the apostles." Yet notice how quickly he moved, in verse 10, to talking about the grace of God. It was by this grace that he said, "I am what I am."

God's grace is real. To pretend that grace is nonexistent or less than it is would be arrogant indeed. That would be to say that God's grace is nothing rather than a significant something. It would be to say that God's grace is in "vain," or for nothing.

Paul's next phrase seems to tip to the other side of the tightrope. He said that not only did God's grace "not prove vain, but I labored even more than all of them," that is, the apostles. Now he seems to have gone from being the least of the apostles to being the most active of the apostles. This was arguably true, but was he now vulnerable to the charge of pride? Note that he immediately qualified this with the phrase "yet not I, but the grace of God with me." The reality of God's grace allowed Paul to know who he was and to assert what he had done without falling into arrogance.

Elsewhere we see Paul walking this same tightrope. In Ephesians 3:8 we read, "To me, the very least of all saints, *this grace was given*" (emphasis added). Similarly, we read, "Christ Jesus came into the world to save sinners, among whom I am foremost of all. *Yet for this reason I found mercy*, so that in me as the foremost, Jesus Christ might demonstrate His perfect patience" (1 Tim 1:15-16, emphasis added). In both of these passages Paul confessed the greatness of his sin—but also, because of that great sin, the greatness and reality of God's grace. Notice in the second passage (1 Tim 1:15-16) that Paul moved from being the "foremost" of sinners to being the "foremost" example of Christ's patience.

We walk another tightrope in dealing with knowledge. We may ask, "Doesn't knowledge lead to pride, division and dryness?" The answer is "Sometimes." Remember, though, that an argument against abuse is not an argument against use. First Corinthians 8:1-3 says, "We all have knowledge. Knowledge makes arrogant, but love edifies. If anyone supposes that he knows anything, he has not yet known as he ought to know; but if anyone loves God, he is known by Him."

It is said that "a little learning is a dangerous thing." Helmut Thielicke emphasizes this very point in his *Little Exercise for Young Theologians*. The great temptation of studying the Bible, theology or ethics is to feel that, because you know more than others, you are better than others. In fact, pride is almost inevitable at an initial stage of learning. You might try to prove your superiority by impressing others or by pushing your point of view down their throats. The antidote to this "little learning" is not to stop learning but to go from a little learning to a lot of learning.

The 1 Corinthians 8 passage emphasizes that if you suppose you know anything, you have not yet known as you ought to know. In other words, the more you know, the more you know that you don't know. Augustine argued that there are in the Bible "shallows in which lambs can wade and depths in which elephants can swim." We will never come close to exhausting our knowledge of the Bible, much less the God of the Bible. We also need to use our knowledge for the edification of others ("love edifies") and in order to love God and be known by him.

Luther once said, "Human nature is like a drunken peasant. Lift him into the saddle on one side, over he topples on the other side."[1] Whether you prefer the picture of the tightrope or the drunken peasant, we as humans are always tending toward despair because of our own failure and inadequacy or toward falling off the other side, into pride. Knowledge can lead to humility or arrogance. It is possible, though not easy, to keep our balance, asserting the truth we have discovered as a result of God's grace without being arrogant.

THE NEED FOR ASSERTIONS

The struggle to give a place for religious and ethical assertions without being arrogant is not a new issue. Erasmus and Luther exchanged arguments on this subject in the sixteenth century. The scholar Erasmus (1466?–1536), concerned that our knowledge of Scripture is somewhat obscure and uncertain, said we ought to hesitate to make assertions. Luther responded rather strongly: "It is a pestilent dictum of the Sophists, that the Scriptures are obscure and equivocal." Luther further said, "Take away assertions and you take away Christianity. The truths that he burns on our hearts are twice as inflexible as the Stoics. The Holy Spirit is no skeptic."[2]

Luther was aware, however, of his own fallibility and was open to arguments. The controversy over assertions led to a series of debates with leading theologians such as Johann Eck (1486–1543) and Cajetan (1469–1534). At Augsburg, Luther said, "I have sought after truth in my public disputations, and everything that I have said I still consider as right, true, and Christian. Yet I am but a man, and may be deceived. I am therefore willing to receive instruction and correction in those things wherein I may have erred."[3]

At a meeting in Worms in 1521, with Emperor Charles V present, Luther was asked whether he would recant part or all of his books. He asked for a day to consider this. The next day, when repeatedly pressed to recant, Luther finally responded with these words: "Unless convinced by Scripture or evident reason, I will not, I cannot recant. My conscience is captive to the Word of God. To go against conscience is neither right nor safe. Here I stand, I can do no other, God help me. Amen."[4]

It is important to underline here that believers' assertions about the revelation of God are not necessarily arrogant. Something intrinsic to the gospel makes it either *the* way or *no* way. If the central events of Jesus' life are not as described in the Bible, then Jesus is not even *one* way to God. It is possible to state the claims of the gospel in an arrogant manner, but the truth claim itself is not intrinsically arrogant. It is also important to distinguish between first and second things, to determine the degree of emphasis to place on each aspect of our faith. The motto of the denomination of which I am part is drawn from a saying of Richard Baxter (1615–1691): "In things essential, unity; in nonessentials, liberty; and in all things, charity." It is love that keeps truth from becoming arrogant.

BE FAIR

Here is a guideline to help you guard against arrogance in conversation: be able to state the other person's position to his or her satisfaction before you respond to it. To live by this rule may be time consuming, but it is the only way to be fair as well as effective in responding to alternative views.

I went to a theological seminary where the doctrines denied by professors (sometimes with vehemence) included the Trinity, the deity of Christ, the sinlessness of Christ, the substitutionary atonement, the physical resurrection of Christ, the ascension and Christ's second coming. On top of this there was a great deal of criticism of the Old and New Testaments. In some classes you learned more about the critical methods than about the Bible. The temptation of various students who disagreed with the professors' views was to speak up as soon as they heard something they regarded as error. In most cases this was not effective in persuading the professor or the class of their views. In fact, many times they were made to look like fools because they had not sufficiently studied the views they were countering. Those who made effective responses did so only after much study that enabled them to put their finger on the Achilles' heel of the rival position. These people studied the whole position so that when they pulled out their trump card, the trick was theirs.

I would likewise advise those in universities, graduate schools and seminaries that are antagonistic to orthodox Christianity not to speak up too quickly. When you speak, you want it to be of value to the professor and the class, not just a self-assertion to vindicate your conscience. Listen carefully to the views being taught, study their foundational assumptions and find where the view is vulnerable. Often I found that the same professors who were openly dismissive of classic orthodoxy and proclaimed their views as the only intelligent alternative in class were aware, when confronted in private, about the weakness of their position. Yet they gave no indication of this uncertainty in class. If the right question is asked in class, it may provide an opportunity for the weakness of the opposing position to come out.

It is good to be able to state the other person's position to his or her satisfaction not only so that you might more effectively counter it but also to be fair. We value the dignity of people made in the image of God. When you counter someone in a dismissive, hostile or belligerent manner, you violate his dignity. Even when you do not particularly respect the person you are talking to, it is important to value the image of God in her. James 3:9-10 argues, in effect, that we cannot go to church and bless God, then walk out the next minute and curse someone made in the image and likeness of God. There is a relationship between the worth you ascribe to God and the worth you ascribe to people made in his image. As we have seen, our call is to love not only our neighbor but also our enemy. It is essential that we bend over backwards to be fair to people we oppose. If we are not stating their position accurately, we want to be able to do so.

Stating the others' position to their satisfaction is also good because we may learn something in the process. One of the doctrines particularly developed by Calvin, and later amplified by others, is the idea of "common grace," referring to the gifts that God spreads to all persons regardless of their submission to or rebellion against him. Those gifts include intellectual insights. In his *Institutes* Calvin wrote:

> What then? Shall we deny that the truth shone upon the ancient jurists who established civic order and discipline with such great equity? Shall we say that the philosophers were blind in their fine observation and artful description of nature? Shall we say that those men were devoid of understanding that conceived the art of disputation and taught us to speak reasonably? Shall we say that they are insane who developed medicine, devoting their labor to our benefit? What shall we say of all the mathematical sciences? Shall we consider them the ravings of madmen? No, we cannot read the writings of the ancients on these subjects without great admiration. We marvel at them because we are compelled to recognize how preeminent they are. But shall we count anything praiseworthy or noble without recognizing at the same time that it *comes from God*? Let us be ashamed of such ingratitude. Those men whom Scripture calls "natural men" were indeed sharp and penetrating in their investigation of things below. Let us accordingly learn by their example *how many gifts the Lord left to human nature even after it was despoiled of its true good.*[5]

In his commentary on Genesis, Calvin ascribed many human actions and advances to the work of the Holy Spirit:

For the invention of the arts, and of other things which serve to the common use and convenience of life, is a gift from God by no means to be despised, and a faculty worthy of communication . . . as the experience of all ages teaches us how widely the rays of divine light have shone on unbelieving nations, for the benefit of the present life; and we see at the present time that the *excellent gifts of the Spirit* are diffused through the whole human race.[6]

Far from being narrow in his perspective and unappreciative of pagan thought, he was willing to value all truth as God's truth.

In a similar manner to Calvin's point, we can learn from nonbelieving professors. Many times, reading postmodern, New Age or neopagan literature, I have found true insights that expanded my perspective on the world and even on Christ and the Bible. I have been forced to ask questions of the Scriptures that I might not have asked before. In reading New Age literature I have been stimulated to think about right- and left-brain learning—rational and cognitive as well as imaginative and creative. In reading neopagan critiques of Christian views on the environment, I have been forced to see more clearly how some believers have abused the earth and to appreciate even more the biblical view of creation and its preservation. In many ways these views show the failure of the church to communicate a full-orbed, comprehensive demonstration of the reality of Christ in thought and life. (Now, of course, even the attempt to put forth such a perspective is thought to be arrogant and oppressive.) It is not that the church has tried in most cases to put forward a comprehensive perspective and failed; it is that the view put forward has all too often been narrow, ineffectual and inadequate.

God has given the church enough of the top-drawer intellects of the ages to show that faith in Christ is credible and persuasive, but not so many that we might presume. If believers cannot answer the cultural, philosophical and theological questions of our day, it will be the first time in two thousand years. The great stumbling block now, as it was in the first century, is pride. In 1 Corinthians, Paul said,

Jews ask for signs and Greeks search for wisdom; but we preach Christ crucified, to Jews a stumbling block and to Gentiles foolishness. . . . But God has chosen the foolish things of the world to shame the wise, and God has chosen the weak things of the world to shame the things which are strong, and the base things of the world and the despised God has chosen, the things that are not, that He may nullify the things that are, that no man may boast before God. (1:22-29)

It is this turning upside down of the pride and pretensions of this world that is a key to understanding the power and wisdom of Christ. The gospel calls us to admit our need for salvation to come from another (Christ) and not to come from ourselves. No amount of persuasion can humble the will, although it can clear away obstacles in the mind. It is not only our arguments but also our attitude that is crucial. We need to demonstrate in thought and in life the truth, goodness and beauty of Christ. Being fair to opposing positions is a good start.

THE FINE LINE

As we have seen, there is a fine line between confidence and arrogance. We can be confident, but we cannot be either arrogant or hesitant. What can keep us up on the tightrope or keep us from falling off the horse like the drunken peasant? I would suggest that the answer is wisdom. Wisdom, as defined in Scripture, demonstrates both humility and a power to speak clearly and decisively.

What is wisdom? The Hebrew term *hokmah*—the Old Testament word for wisdom—has three levels of meaning.

First, *hokmah* means a concrete skill for living. It involves knowledge, but it is more than knowledge. You can have much knowledge and have no wisdom. But you need to have knowledge in order to gain wisdom. The New Testament verse that sums up the process most clearly is Hebrews 5:14: "Solid food is for the mature, who because of practice have their senses trained to discern good and evil." We need knowledge (solid food) put into practice so that it leads to discernment or wisdom. The first level of meaning for *hokmah*, then, involves skill. It could be technical (see Ex 28:3), artistic (see Ex 31:3 and 36:1-2) or administrative skill (see 1 Kings 3:16-28). It could be merely social skills, like dealing with marriage and family issues, using money wisely or having discernment in friendships.

The second level of *hokmah* is to know the way the created order works, understanding the structure of reality. Proverbs 25:2 says,

It is the glory of God to conceal a matter,
But the glory of kings is to search out a matter.

We search and discover the hidden treasures God has left for us to find. In Proverbs 1—9 we are called to see how things work, eschewing wrong friendships (those that offer bad influences) and avoiding adultery. Often the contrast in these chapters is between "Lady Wisdom," calling out for us to hear her, competing with the other lady—the adulteress. In both cases Scripture shows the end of the road, the inevitable consequences of following that path, whether life or destruction. We are to internalize this knowledge of the external order.

The third level of *hokmah* (once we have gained all the tools) is creativity with respect to life. For instance, my wife took piano lessons for many years and can now play any song or composition without music or chords, because the structure of the chords is embedded within her. Someone can improvise with jazz only after much musical training and listening to jazz. Anyone is "free" to win the U.S. Open Tennis Tournament, but without many years of training his or her instincts to hit all kinds of shots, a player will not make it very far in the tournament. Without the initial discipline, our options are few. Once the foundational disciplines are established, then we experience the freedom for creativity.[7] We can only have the creativity to respond to a variety of people and issues clearly and yet humbly if we gain wisdom.

OPEN-MINDED

Wisdom starts with the fear of the Lord (see Prov 1:7; 8:13; 9:10; 15:33). The more we revere God, the more we are stripped of our pride and self-delusion. We see our finitude and fallenness. This awareness that we have much to learn makes us teachable. In order to be wise we must be teachable. Proverbs 15:31 says,

> He whose ear listens to the life-giving reproof
> Will dwell among the wise.

Proverbs 21:11 affirms,

> When the wise is instructed,
> he receives knowledge.

And Proverbs 17:10 teaches,

> A rebuke goes deeper into one who has understanding
> Than a hundred blows into a fool.

This means that the wise are always open-minded, ready to receive knowledge wherever it comes from—although with discernment.

SPIRITUAL ENTROPY

As long as we keep on listening and learning, we can continue to gain wisdom. Once we stop listening, things tend toward disorder, as with the thermodynamic law of entropy. Solomon started out as the wisest of kings, but in his later life he did some very unwise things. How was this possible? I believe that he forgot the teaching ascribed to him (see Prov 10:1), as recorded in Proverbs 19:27:

> Cease listening, my son, to discipline,
> And you will stray from the words of knowledge.

If you "cease to listen," you will "stray." Perhaps we all know those who seemed wise but who have done foolish, life-altering things. In many cases they fell in private before they fell in public. Spiritual entropy took over when they ceased listening to wisdom.

True wisdom is both assertive and humble. The tongue has great power. "Death and life are in the power of the tongue" (Prov 18:21). An order given by a terrorist leader can lead to the deaths of many. Many people in public life have lost their jobs and reputations over a slip of the tongue.

A fool's mouth is his ruin,
And his lips are the snare of his soul. (Prov 18:7)

So wisdom knows when to speak and how to speak. Sometimes silence is better than speaking. "Even a fool, when he keeps silent, is considered wise" (Prov 17:28). And "he who restrains his words has knowledge" (v. 27). Wisdom can give us an apt answer—

A man has joy in an apt answer,
And how delightful is a timely word! (15:23)

The Lord can show us how to answer—

The plans of the heart belong to man,
But the answer of the tongue is from the LORD. (16:1)

The power of the tongue is great, but not too great for godly wisdom to tame it.

We are not going to consistently make assertions without arrogance unless we have gained wisdom. One of my favorite Old Testament passages says,

The Lord GOD has given me the tongue of disciples,
That I may know how to sustain the weary one with a word.
He awakens me morning by morning,
He awakens my ear to listen as a disciple.
The Lord GOD has opened My ear;
And I was not disobedient. (Is 50:4-5)

This is one of the Servant passages of Isaiah that point to Christ. It would indeed be marvelous if we gained a wise tongue—what the Revised Standard Version calls the "tongue of those who are taught"—so that we could speak the right word at the right time in the right way. We could not only help the "weary one" but also give wise responses to other issues.

How can we gain this wise tongue? The passage indicates that it is "morning by morning" being taught by the Lord, having him "awaken my ear to listen." Whether it is morning by morning, afternoon by afternoon or evening by evening, we need to gain wisdom, for only to the extent that we gain wisdom can we walk the tightrope between arrogance and hesitance and have the ability to make assertions about true truth without arrogance.

INFALLIBLE ABSOLUTES,
FALLIBLE PEOPLE

BILL: *Okay, maybe some Christians speak out against arrogance, but what about the fact that we are so limited in the amount of knowledge we have? Our perspective is shaped by our culture. History is fiction. There are no facts, only interpretations. There is no objective view of reality. Anybody telling you otherwise is just putting a spin on the facts because of their own vested interests.*

JOHN: *Wow! You have been reading a lot in the postmodern philosophy.*

BILL: *What do you say to their position? Do you just turn a blind eye to it?*

JOHN: *No, there are many points where I would agree with postmodern emphases. I'm not a modernist. Yet there are, as you might have guessed, points where I disagree.*

⌒⌒⌒

G. K. Chesterton once observed, "There is something to be said for every error, but whatever may be said for it, the most important thing to be said about it is that it is erroneous."[1] This is certainly true of postmodernism. While we should acknowledge its positive aspects, we also must hold the line against it where it is wrong.

Perhaps no two people would agree completely on any definition of "modernism" and "postmodernism." Generally, though, modernism is considered to be a way of thinking that reigned in the West since the Renaissance or at least since the Enlightenment. It emphasizes such things as rationality, order, coherence, unity and power. Postmodernism is an alternative way of thinking that has come on strong only since the mid-twentieth century. Consciously rejecting its predecessor, postmodernism emphasizes emotion, diversity and mystery, refusing to paper over the differences among people. Relativism of many kinds fits well with postmodernism.

While we can be opponents of some of the extreme positions of postmodernists, we can also learn many truths and insights from them. There is "something to be said" for them, in Chesterton's words. At best postmodernism might be considered a meditation on the finitude and fallibility of our knowledge. As believers, we know we have infallible absolutes in Scripture, and yet we are finite, fallen people. What we can learn about ourselves from postmodernists, if we listen, is that too often we give the impression that we "know it all," have infinite knowledge or have absolute knowledge of *all* the absolutes.

Yes, we understand that we need to find only one absolute in order to reject relativism. And this we can do. But the fact remains that any view that gains a widespread following usually has emphasized a number of truths that resonate with people. Most especially, postmodernism has rightly criticized the arrogance and pretensions of modernism. In this chapter we want to examine some of the valid insights of postmodernism as well as point to some of the ways it goes astray.

All Truth Is God's Truth

Some Christians resist the idea that we can learn anything from "those who are in error." Yet it is good to learn everything we can about anything we can because each particular truth will lead us inevitably back to the God of truth. All truth is God's truth. We can afford to admit truth where we see it. Theologian B. B. Warfield (1851–1921) wrote:

> We must not, then, as Christians, assume an antagonism towards the truths of reason, or the truths of philosophy, or the truths of science, or the truths of history, or the truths of criticism. As children of the light, we must be careful to keep ourselves open to every ray

of light. . . . Let us, then, cultivate an attitude of courage as over against the investigations of the day. None should be more zealous in them than we. None should be quicker to discern truth in every field, more hospitable to receive it, more loyal to follow it, whithersoever it leads. It is not for Christians to be lukewarm in regard to the investigations and discoveries of the time. Rather as followers of the Truth indeed we can have no safety in science or in philosophy, save in the arms of truth. It is for us as Christians to push investigation to the utmost; to be leaders on every science; to stand in the van [forefront] of criticism; to be the first to catch in every field, the voice of the Revealer of truth, who is also our Redeemer. The curse of the Church has been her apathy to truth, in which she has left to her enemies that study of nature and of history and of philosophy, and even that investigation of her own peculiar treasures, the Scriptures of God, which should have been her chief concern. . . . She has nothing to fear from truth; but she has everything to fear, and has already suffered nearly everything, from ignorance. All truth belongs to us as followers of Christ, the Truth; let us at length enter into our inheritance.[2]

Although we can be fearless in investigating the discoveries of our time, we also need to be discerning. There is both honey and hemlock in books we read—and I am speaking of both Christian and non-Christian books when I say this.

What is right and what is wrong with postmodernism? Here is a sketch of the issues.

WHAT IS POSTMODERNISM?

Jean-François Lyotard (1907–1998), professor of philosophy, defined postmodernism as "incredulity toward metanarratives." Lyotard was suspicious of any story or account of the world that claimed to be absolute or all-encompassing—a metanarrative. Postmodernists are suspicious not only because of the limits of reason but also because such perspectives have been oppressive. Therefore, Lyotard, a deconstructionist, said we must take apart all metanarratives.

David Lehman, in *Signs of the Times* (a brilliant and playful look at deconstructionism), suggested that we could eliminate the letters c-o-n from this philosophical approach and call it by its real name: *destructionism*. Lyotard and others of his ilk believe in the destruction of any objective knowledge of reality, morality, literature or anything else. Or, Lehman suggested, we could also place the accent on the syllable "con" and say that any attempt to affirm knowledge is a con.

More seriously, various postmodernists affirm the following:

- There is no objective view of reality. We are shaped by our culture. We can have "objectivity" by our cultural standards but no transcultural or supracultural objectivity.
- Because we are so culturally determined, we cannot judge another culture.
- There are no facts, only interpretations. (Nietzsche)
- History is fiction. History is written from the perspective of the culture, race or gender of the writer. What is "historic" is totally subjective. It depends on the bias of the writer. (Foucault)
- Knowledge is power. We ought to be suspicious of any who claim to give us truth. They are out to further their own (and their group's) vested interests. (Foucault)
- Ethical claims are mere sentiment. There are, for instance, no neutral grounds to condemn the Holocaust. (Rorty)
- Deconstruction is justice. We ought to explore and find the contradictions in every piece of literature so that we can uphold justice and avoid injustice. (Derrida)
- Whoever "spins" best wins. Since there is no objective truth, all we have is rhetoric. Whoever plays the game best wins. Make sure it is you. (Fish)

FAITH AND REASON

In the form of an equation in which F stands for faith and R stands for reason, postmodernism could be compared and contrasted with other views as follows:

R − F = M (modernism or rationalism)
F − R = F (fideism, or "faithism")
F + R = C (classical apologetics)
−F − R = P (postmodernism)

Postmodernism is the end of the line: there is no objective faith and no objective reason.

Here is another analogy that might help us understand the differences in views. In this analogy a tree represents faith and reason in full flower (see figure 5.1). Some views might hack off branches (discard certain arguments); others might dwarf the tree (reason is of some value but not much); still others would chop the tree off at the trunk (no apologetic allowed). But that's not all. Others would dig up the roots (critique all foundational assumptions), and finally, others would cement the hole so that nothing will ever grow there again (postmodernism).

WE AGREE

Certainly there are some points on which we could agree with postmodern philosophers. Among them are the following:

There are limits to knowledge. Reason cannot develop a comprehensive knowledge of reality. There is much about reality that is mysterious and defies neat categories of description. In the realms of imagination, experience and practice, there is much that goes beyond our ability to describe adequately in words. The postmodernists' critique of the pretensions of rationalism (modernism) has much to commend it.

Your perspective does affect what you see. If you stand on top of one mountain, it will look different from how it would look if you stood on top of another mountain. If you rigorously analyze life, you will see only a part of it. Our cultural vantage point differs from that of another. Faith in Christ is not necessarily Western or Eastern. We can afford to be truly multicultural and diverse. After all, do we not see an ultimate vision in

Revelation 5:9 of people from every tribe, tongue, people and nation? Such diverse people worship the same Lord. Surely this is a great Lord Jesus. No one culture has the corner on truth or on Jesus.

Figure 5.1 Faith and reason in full flower

Our perspective affects the way we view history. What we view as "historic," as opposed to the merely historical flow of events, will be determined by what we regard as important. Our cultural perspective does affect what we see in history. The questions we ask of history function like a stencil placed over the mass of events. The shape of our stencil determines what we see. People in African American studies and feminist historians have rightly pointed out the virtual exclusion of blacks and women from many historical accounts. We need to be open to questioning the values by which we determine what is historic. This, however, does not mean that all history is fiction.

My ideas of God and reality are too small. My ideas sometimes need to be smashed so that I can gain a better view of reality. Very often "your God is too small," as J. B. Phillips maintained in his book by that title. We need to continually stretch our understanding of our Lord. Similarly, we sometimes need to smash our limiting concepts of things or people so that we can think outside our previous box. What I need is not my idea of my wife, but my wife. What I need is not my idea of my boys, but my boys. We continually need to revise our inadequate or outmoded concepts.

Culture can blind us to some aspects of who we are. We can unthinkingly take for granted certain cultural assumptions, unless they are questioned. The classic illustration is the frog in the kettle. If you put a frog in a kettle of water and turn up the heat, the frog adjusts to the rising temperature and therefore does not try to jump out until it is too late. In a similar way we can be affected by our cultural environment and yet be unaware of the significant impact being made upon us. In Colossians 2:8 we are warned to beware of philosophy. Some believers have used this as a pretext for avoiding the subject altogether, but the only way to *beware* of philosophy is to *be aware* of it. In any case, we can agree that we can be culturally shortsighted and therefore, as a corrective attempt, expose ourselves to people from other cultures and earlier ages.

WE DISAGREE

Despite the helpful reminders of postmodernists in some areas, we would certainly disagree with many of the positions they take, especially their conviction that there is no objective knowledge of truth or morality.

Many postmodern contentions are self-refuting. We might ask, is it objectively true to say that there are no objective truths? Can you deny the validity of reason without using reason? If "all perspectives of reality are culturally determined," then is this statement itself culturally determined or transcultural? If all metanarratives are suspect because they lead to oppression, then can it not be maintained that postmodernism is itself a metanarrative and equally suspect? If all knowledge claims are a grab for power, then are not postmodernism's contentions equally motivated by a will to power?

We can see this regarding the views of Karl Marx (1818–1883) and Sigmund Freud (1856–1939), grandfathers of postmodernism. If all philosophies are economically motivated, as Marx said, what about Marx's own philosophy? If all belief comes out of the nonrational unconscious, as Freud would have it, then is this not true of Freud's own views?

Are postmodernists sawing off the branch they are sitting on? I think so. Interestingly, one postmodern writer, Jonathan Culler, picked up this image in his book *On Deconstruction* and said, yes, he is sawing off the branch, but there is no ground to fall onto.[3] Maybe not, but a call to the paramedics might be wise.

Suspicion can work both ways. The psychological charge "Christianity is a crutch" might be answered by the countercharge that "atheism is a crutch." In a similar way postmodernism is, à la Marx, an opiate of the conscience or, à la Freud, a grand Oedipus complex wishing the death of the heavenly Father. The suspicion that Freud directed at individuals' motives, postmodernists direct at the whole culture. Perhaps they need to suspect their own suspicions along with all of the other suspicions.

Postmodernism's moral conclusions deserve suspicion. A view maintaining that there is no "neutral ground" on which we can condemn something like the Holocaust deserves suspicion. Some feminists (not Christian believers) maintain that radical relativism actually perpetuates oppression and injustice toward women because it makes words like *justice* and *injustice* mere emotive terms.[4]

The view that cultures differ so widely that there is no common moral ground is false. In recent years the patron saint of cultural relativism, anthropologist Margaret Mead (1901–1978), has come under a withering critique by Derek Freeman in his book *Margaret Mead and Samoa.* The book raises profound questions about the scholarship and honesty of this popularizer of what has become the foundational assumption of postmodernism. C. S. Lewis said about this belief: "The pretence that we are presented with a mere chaos—as though no outline of universally accepted value shows through—is simply false and should be contradicted in season and out of season wherever it is met."[5] Lewis and others make a persuasive case for values that transcend culture.[6]

We can diametrically oppose the manner in which deconstructionists approach an author's text. One postmodern professor wanted to destroy his students' love of literature. Characteristically, postmodernism embodies an emphasis on standing over texts and "interrogating" them, that is, reading between the lines and reading against the grain. Postmodernists are suspicious of the racist, sexist, ethnocentric motives of the various authors they interrogate.

By contrast, we can receive literature. We can love seeing the world through others' eyes and love worlds that people like J. R. R. Tolkien or C. S. Lewis invent.

When you receive a great story, there is a sense of getting out of yourself and getting into another's world. Thus there is a connection between literature and love. When we love, we put ourselves in another's place, attempting to see the world as he or she does. We transcend our self-centeredness. Here is a more perfect love that casts out fear.

The question persists about postmodernism (despite its protests to embrace other cultures): Does its methodology of suspicion, fear and criticism make it, in the end, incapable of loving? Does its fear cast out love?

Many postmodern claims are partial truths exaggerated into the whole truth. Postmodernists exaggerate the problem of objectivity; they exaggerate the difficulty of interpretation; and they exaggerate the difficulty of crosscultural communication. Certainly the claim to absolutes can become oppressive, but the denial of absolutes could lead to an even greater oppression.

Above all, we need caution about tying our methods too closely to a passing trend like postmodernism. If we buy into the latest fashion in philosophy, it may go out of fashion soon. Only that which is timeless and eternal remains forever relevant.

It is difficult for us to believe that the newest is not the best. In this day of cell phones, CDs and DVDs, we quickly learn the value of new technology. What will the next generation of technology bring?

This desire for the newest and latest is not only a powerful drive in twenty-first century technology but it can be a drive in the realm of ideas and values as well. Many voices in the contemporary educational establishment proclaim that the newest is the best. We are tempted to follow the newest philosophy, read the newest books and come up with a novel perspective as our own. This temptation needs further consideration.

Theologian Thomas Oden is a model in this regard. Earlier in his life he was a respected, published liberal theologian. Once when leaving on a sabbatical, he could take only a limited number of books. He was shocked when he looked at the books he had chosen. None of the newest fad theologies were included, only old classics. Gradually he worked his way back to "mere Christianity." Oden had a dream in which he saw his own tombstone on which was written, "He contributed nothing new." As he thought about this, he came to see that novelty had consumed his life up until then. He determined in his life and in his new theology series to "teach nothing new."[7] He found it necessary to resist the thrust of his education in order "to overcome the constant temptation to novelty."[8]

An ancient proverb maintains, "What is true is not new and what is new is not true." While we certainly can and should try to unearth new insight from the Scriptures, we need to be cautious if our new nuggets differ radically from views held in the past. Perhaps those past views need correction and we are the ones to do it. However, if we greatly differ from the giants of the faith, we need to be open to the possibility that it is we, not they, who need correction.

It is not necessarily wrong to contribute a novel perspective in our field, but it is best not to seek novelty or originality as an end in itself. Being original is not the main purpose of life. Originality or novelty is best sought indirectly (by doing good work) rather than directly. Then you may stumble onto originality without trying. The danger is trying too hard to be something you are not rather than letting your originality flow out of who you are.

We can agree with the postmodern emphasis on the finitude of knowledge and the complexity of reality. However, we should not forsake reasoning with postmodernists firmly but gently. "Does this not make sense?" "What do you think about this?" "Don't you see where this leads?" Perhaps we can also tell stories and use metaphors. Often we see the meaning of something more clearly through the imagination than by abstract reasoning. Good stories can point us toward a clearer view of reality.

It is important to emphasize here that our perspective is finite and limited because we are creatures created by God. Only God has an infinite view of reality. At its best postmodernism is a meditation on the finitude of our knowledge. While we disagree with the extreme implications postmodernists draw, we can strongly agree that we are limited in many respects. We are given a revelation of infallible absolutes, but we are finite people.

INFALLIBLE ABSOLUTES, FALLEN SITUATIONS

BILL: *In light of what you have agreed with in postmodernism, why is it that so many Christians seem "black and white," especially in politics?*

JOHN: *National life is important. Not surprisingly, it generates passion. Certainly believers want to speak to what is a good law as opposed to a bad law, and that requires clear moral standards. However, applying truth to the complex context of politics is often not so easy.*

BILL: *Now you are sounding like me. Maybe I am winning you over to relativism.*

JOHN: *I believe that the Scriptures contain clear moral standards—absolutes—that can help us orient ourselves in politics, but the struggle is in relating those principles to complex issues and the process of compromise in politics. Just because you believe in some absolutes doesn't mean that all your positions are predetermined.*

ⓖⓜⓢⓟ

We have infallible absolutes in Scripture, but we encounter fallen situations that are so complex that it is difficult to know which way to go. This is particularly the case in politics. In some debates believers honestly differ on the best course to take, and it is difficult to say which position is better. In other cases the moral principles are clear but the matter of getting a law through the political process dilutes its purity. Believers are sometimes caricatured as "black and white," admitting no ambiguities in life. How do we deal with agonizing circumstances where various absolutes seem to conflict and where we need to settle for less than we want?

THE POLITICAL ILLUSION

Not long ago people like prominent evangelical theologian Carl Henry had to call believers to involvement in social and political causes.[1] The call was to play the role of salt and light in the society. The pendulum has, however, swung to the other side—and then a little bit back. Some believers, heeding this call to involvement in politics, plunged in with fervor. But when their side won, they were disappointed to find that utopia did not arrive, heaven was not brought to earth. Some became disillusioned with the seeming lack of results when reality did not measure up to their expectations.

The danger is always to expect too much or too little from political involvement. A book in my library has a title that speaks volumes: *Everything Is Politics, but Politics Is Not Everything*. It is especially important to emphasize the phrase "politics is not everything" because those who live in the Washington, D.C., area are under the temptation to believe that politics *is* everything. It is rightly said that "power corrupts and absolute power corrupts absolutely." In a similar way it can be observed that *closeness to power* corrupts as well. One godly leader had an opportunity to move to Washington, D.C., to pursue ministry and decided not to do it because he did not think he could handle the spiritual temptation of closeness to power.

In his book *Kingdoms in Conflict,* former White House adviser Chuck Colson reflected on those believers in the Nixon years who gained an audience with the president. They had all kinds of important agendas to pursue and criticisms to make while in the waiting room, but when they were allowed into the Oval Office with the president, they muted their concerns or did not mention them at all. What if they were not invited back? What if they lost their access to power? Closeness to power corrupted the ability to speak clearly about what they believed.

Added to this temptation is the reality that politics can only do so much. It can only set the basic tone of the country, establishing the lowest common denominator of behavior that will be allowed. The bar is not set very high. Politicians can use the bully pulpit to call people higher, but they cannot make people moral beings. Samuel Johnson once made a wise remark:

How small of all that human hearts endure,
that part which king or laws can cause or cure.

Politicians and laws cannot touch many of the deep spiritual issues in the human heart. _politics not solution to all_

POLITICAL MANDATES

On the other hand, it would be a disaster if people of faith withdrew from the public sector. Richard Neuhaus's book *The Naked Public Square* makes this argument. In politics it is important to discern the difference between a good and a bad law. Where do most people get the basis on which to make this kind of judgment? Is it not from faith-based morality? Should we let relativism decide what is a good or bad law? On what basis could that decision be made? Personal preference or sentiment?

When it comes down to it, there are only four foundations for law: absolutes, anarchy, majority rule and totalitarianism.[2]

In the first case, law can be based on universal fixed standards—absolutes. The founders of this country seem to have intended this in the Declaration of Independence. They held to inalienable rights granted by the Creator, namely the rights to "life, liberty, and the pursuit of happiness." What could provide the basis for an inalienable right? It would have to be one that is not arbitrary or able to be taken away even if the majority in the country says so. In other words, these rights are not "alienable." This preamble to the Constitution seems to provide a framework through which the Constitution can be interpreted (though sometimes the Declaration of Independence and the Constitution have been divorced from each other). In any case the Founders seemed to believe that rights from the Creator provided a safeguard to preserve human dignity.

The second logical option as a basis for law is anarchy. In this option everybody creates their own rules and does whatever they want. Each individual will reigns supreme, and there is no basis to judge among competing wills. (Such a prospect is not very palatable and thus this view is held by few.)

The third option is held by many: majority rules. This option is also called "positive law." It was put forward by Supreme Court justice Oliver Wendell Holmes (1841–1935). In this view the majority determines by vote what is right. In our system we can vote occasionally on some laws in a direct fashion. Most of the laws made are through our elected representatives at the local, state or national levels. This view works well as long as the populace is informed by fixed rules drawn from their faith. But what if a majority wanted to do away with the rights of humans to "life, liberty, and the pursuit of happiness"? What if a majority in the future determined that first-degree murder was allowable by law? On what ground could this be opposed? In this view there is no higher ground than the majority.

The final view, the totalitarian option, puts the determination of law into one person's hands or into the hands of a ruling elite. This is certainly not the most preferable option because our experience in history has shown that this has led to horrible abuses. People given absolute power have tended to be corrupted by it. The "wise king" idea was put forward by theologian Thomas Aquinas (1225–1274) as the best government. The problem, though, is finding a perfectly wise king. Because of the Fall, it is in fact unwise to concentrate too much power in one person or group. Democracy is notoriously inefficient, but it is the safest and best alternative available. Someone once said, "Democracy is the worst form of government, except for all the others." We could say that the repressed premise of the American political system is original sin. The rejection of the concentration of power in one individual or even in one branch of government shows skepticism about possible abuses of power. Thus we have a "balance of powers."

In the four views, the roots of law are in God's will (absolutes), each individual's will (anarchy), the majority's will (majority rules) or one person's will or that of a ruling elite (totalitarianism). Once we give up our Founders' perspective, it is far from clear on what basis we ought to predicate law. The de facto basis in many sectors today is "majority rules." In other words, might makes right.

Relativism is a serious danger for such a society. Peter Kreeft argued,

> Even in a secular society like America it is still true that religion is the firmest support for morality. There has never been a popular secular morality that's lasted and worked to hold a society together, society has always needed morality, and morality has always needed religion. Destroy religion, you destroy morality; destroy morality, you destroy society. That's history's bottom line.[3]

If the believer in absolutes deserts the public square, one of the other views will take more influence, probably majority rules. However, to the degree that chaos caused by relativism reigns, people may be willing to sacrifice freedom for security, moving in the totalitarian direction.

THE DIFFICULTY OF POLITICS

Sometimes involvement in politics is difficult for believers, because politics is often defined as "the art of compromise." People of faith do not like compromise; therefore, politics is suspect. Certainly it is never right to go against your conscience and to compromise your principles; however, it is sometimes necessary to settle for less than you desire. It is better to get something rather than nothing. It is better to get half a loaf than no loaf at all.

Even when you know what is right, it is not always easy to see what is wise given the political realities. Often the temptation of believers in politics is to go for it all, risking achieving nothing. Wisdom is needed to know when this is a good strategy and when it is not. In one instance a friend of mine had an opportunity to attach a law to a bill being considered in Congress. The law banned indecent pornography by phone for those under eighteen years of age. It was crafted in reaction to the Supreme Court's fine distinctions of allowing "indecent" pornography but prohibiting "obscene" pornography. Understandably, my friend found both indecent and obscene pornography offensive and wrong. As it was an election year and few congressional representatives wanted to face their electorate appearing soft on pornography, the bill passed, despite fierce backroom opposition. Unfortunately, two years later the Supreme Court struck down the law nine to zero. My friend was left wondering if the law would still be on the books had it asked for less. In this case he went for it all and ended up with nothing. Here is the agonizing tension between principle (pornography of any kind is morally objectionable) and political reality (the law allows more than we might desire).

What should a believer's stance have been in this case? It is not easy to say. Believers might differ over how to respond to this situation.

In a conversation with a highly placed official in government, I learned of the real frustrations such officials face. You might think that attaining a position of political power would allow you to accomplish a good deal of your agenda, yet this person lamented that all too often the best ideas either get stuck in Capitol Hill committees or get increasingly diluted as they go through the political process. Many people add to or subtract from the original bill, resulting in a piece of legislation that may be substantially different from the original. It can be discouraging. However, what would our nation be like if believers absented themselves from the political process? The situation would certainly be worse than it is.

It is not always clear to believers which position is right. There are also cases where sincere believers differ on what position to take. You can listen to both sides of the issues and see the question from both perspectives. Even when we know clearly what is right, it is not always clear how to persuade others in a pluralistic society, and it is certainly not easy to negotiate the give-and-take compromises of the political process.

We need humility as we face complex dilemmas in life and in politics. When I told someone I was working on a book on truth, this person responded, "I think truth is both absolute and relative." As we discussed this comment further, it became clear that this person believed that the truth of Christ was that which was the absolute, eternal and timeless part. The "relative" part was *relating* truth to the complexities of life. I pointed out that there is a difference between relativism, which maintains that everything is relative, and the need to relate truth to the complexities of reality. Although having eternal truth is of great value in sorting out issues, it does not make everything easy or "black and white."

Let us remember: We need humility, prayer and a willingness to listen to various perspectives in order to make wise decisions in life.

DEFENSE WITHOUT DEFENSIVENESS

BILL: *Usually when I have this kind of discussion, Christians get so defensive that they don't seem to hear anything I'm saying.*

JOHN: *No they don't! OK, just kidding. Why do you think they are that way?*

BILL: *Maybe they are insecure.*

JOHN: *Perhaps that is because they are afraid your questions will rock their faith. However, the Bible does not encourage that kind of defensive, fearful attitude. I can see why you are so turned off by it. Fear is the opposite of the love Christ encourages.*

෧෴෧

Too often we believers are defensive, reacting to criticisms quickly—and revealing a deep sense of insecurity about our faith. Sometimes our insecurity is rooted in fear. *What if I cannot find the answer to this person's question? What if this intimidating question is right and my faith cannot stand up under analysis?* Often we are driven by fear in our interactions with the culture.

GIVING A DEFENSE

The classic passage on apologetics is 1 Peter 3:15. Many Christians have heard the call to be "ready to make a defense to everyone who asks." But most have not examined the larger context that shows us the way to make a defense without defensiveness. Peter said,

Even if you should suffer for the sake of righteousness, you are blessed. And do not fear their intimidation, and do not be troubled, but sanctify Christ as Lord in your hearts, always being ready to make a defense to everyone who asks you to give an account for the hope that is in you, yet with gentleness and reverence; and keep a good conscience so that in the thing in which you are slandered, those who revile your good behavior in Christ will be put to shame. For it is better, if God should will it so, that you suffer for doing what is right rather than for doing what is wrong. (1 Pet 3:14-17)

Notice that the context of this passage is the fear of suffering and the consequent danger of being intimidated: "Do not fear their intimidation, and do not be troubled."

It is easy for fear to make us think everything is against us. Fear can be paralyzing. Danish philosopher Søren Kierkegaard (1813–1855) said, "No Grand Inquisitor has in readiness such terrible tortures as anxiety."[1] A little saying puts it well:

Worriers feel every blow
That never falls
And they cry over things
They will never lose.[2]

There is certainly much out there in the world to fear—war, terrorism, rejection, failure and death, to name a few. But not all fear is bad. I distinguish among three types of fear: (1) natural fear, (2) sinful fear and (3) religious fear. Only the second fear is bad.

Natural fear has a life-preserving value. It is good to feel a healthy fear at getting too close to the edge of a cliff, keeping your distance from a wild bear or doing a life-threatening stunt. I read an article once about people without fear. Not surprisingly, they live considerably shorter lives than others. If a wild lion walked into the room where you are sitting, what would happen? Your heart would start pumping faster and adrenaline would start flowing in your system, preparing you for one of two responses—fight or flight. You might throw this book at the lion and head out the nearest exit. Natural fear motivates us to resist threats to life and limb.

It is easy, however, for natural fear to become sinful fear. That happens when natural fear becomes excessive, and it becomes excessive when we give to someone or something the power that only God should have to help us or hurt us. For instance, we can fear someone's disapproval more than God's disapproval, which is to say we can desire their approval more than God's approval. In effect, then, that person becomes a god in our life, having the ultimate power to determine our attitudes and actions.

We can be driven by fear on a cultural level as well as an individual level. Conspiracy theory is as American as apple pie. From books on the assassination of John F. Kennedy to James Bond films to Robert Ludlum novels, the theme of conspiracy is seen everywhere, whether in fantasy or in "reality." Most of these conspiracy theories have little if any truth to them. About a decade ago, a *Publishers Weekly* reporter went to a Christian booksellers convention and claimed that half the books there were driven by fear—fear of the New Age, fear of the Antichrist, fears generated by the "culture wars."[3] As a child I was taught that God and I are a majority in any situation. Even though that may be a little naive (believers do not always win the battle, but they do win the war), it does accent faith in God. Os Guinness said that often believers "talk of standing on the Rock of Ages, but act as if they are clinging to the last piece of driftwood."[4] Paranoia strikes deep in the heart.

Isaiah 8:11-13 speaks directly to this tendency to be driven by fear of conspiracies. (A part of this passage is quoted in 1 Peter 3:14.) The prophet said,

> The LORD spoke to me with mighty power and instructed me not to walk in the way of this people, saying,
>
> You are not to say, "It is a conspiracy!"

In regard to all that this people call a conspiracy,
And you are not to fear what they fear or be in dread of it.
It is the LORD of hosts whom you should regard as holy,
And He shall be your fear,
And He shall be your dread.

We are not to have the same perspective on conspiracies that the general culture does. We are not to fear what the culture does. We are not to be driven by fear at all, except for the fear of God. As the prophetic passage says, "He shall be your fear, and He shall be your dread."

The third kind of fear is religious fear—fear of God. It involves a reverence for and respect toward God. This is not, to use Luther's terminology, a "servile" fear that we might have of a harsh and cruel taskmaster. It is a "filial" fear that a son or daughter might have of a loving father or mother. It is not a fear of rejection by God but a fear of distancing ourselves from God by our behavior or by proving ungrateful for the love God has shown us. At the end of Ecclesiastes all our responsibilities with respect to life are summed up as "fear God and keep His commandments, because this applies to every person" (12:13).

When we rightly fear God, that relativizes sinful fear and keeps it in check. The higher fear drives out the lesser fear. I find that the more I know God at a particular time, the less I fear. Also, the less I know God, the more I fear. The degree of my fears and awareness of other problems is like a thermometer that can tell me where I am in my spiritual life. The Bible says "Fear not" almost ninety times. God must know our tendencies. Martyn Lloyd-Jones once said that much of the problem with our lives is that we "listen to ourselves rather than talk to ourselves."[5] We listen to the fears, anxieties and worries that pop up in the early morning or late at night, rather than saying, "Stop! Remember who God is and his promises to you."

When we are intimidated or afraid, it is easy to be defensive while giving our defense (1 Pet 3:15). How can we avoid this trap?

First Peter 3 says, "Do not fear their intimidation, and do not be troubled, but sanctify Christ as Lord in your hearts" (3:14-15). To sanctify Christ means to set him apart, to regard him as holy, to be in awe of him. It seems that "He shall be your fear, and He shall be your dread" has been transposed to "sanctify Christ." Further, as we sanctify Christ as Lord in our hearts, in reality then he takes the first place as Lord. When we keep first things first, then we can get a clearer perspective on second things. If we know in our mind and heart that Christ is Lord, we can keep our fears in their proper place and approach a reasoned defense with a confident, and not paranoid, manner.

Later Peter said that having sanctified Christ as Lord in our hearts, we will "always [be] ready to make a defense to everyone who asks [us] to give an account of the hope that is in [us]" (1 Pet 3:15). Notice that we are "always" to be ready to make a defense to "everyone" who asks. We all need to be continually prepared. Note also that the word *apologia* means to give an ordered, coherent, thought-through presentation. Sometimes the word is used for a legal brief, sometimes just in a general sense—to give an ordered response.

The defense we are to give is not to be abstracted from our lives but be "an account for the hope in *you*." What has counted most for *you* in believing Christ?

In 2 Corinthians 10:5 Paul gives a summary of our task: "We are destroying speculations and every lofty thing raised up against the knowledge of God, and we are taking every thought captive to the obedience of Christ." The negative task is giving a critique of the reigning philosophies, worldviews and "speculations" that get in the way of people knowing God. The positive task is "taking every thought captive to the obedience of Christ." This last phrase is close in meaning to "sanctify Christ as Lord in your hearts." We take thoughts captive by making Christ Lord.

Our attitude in giving our *apologia* is not to be defensiveness or arrogance but "gentleness and reverence." The word *gentleness,* in the Greek, means meekness, not weakness. Aristotle (384–322 B.C.) defined this

80

word as a mean between getting angry without cause and not getting angry at all. It means "getting angry at the right time, in the right measure, and for the right reason."[6] The word *reverence* in the Greek is the word for fear, meaning either the fear of God or respect for the person you are talking to. It is probably the former in this case. We have a responsibility toward God for the person or people we are talking to. The apostle Paul said to the Ephesian elders, "I am innocent of the blood of all men. For I did not shrink from declaring to you the whole purpose of God" (Acts 20:26-27; see also Ezek 3:17-21).

We have an awesome responsibility before God not to be a stumbling block to people because of wrong ways of speaking, attitudes and actions. The above passages imply that we might not be "innocent" in both our message and our manner, and thus would have to answer to God. Of course, our fear of God will necessarily be translated into respect for people we are engaging. So it probably does not ultimately matter what we refer "reverence" to, God or humankind.

The passage goes on to say that the manner of our life matters a great deal. Our defense can be undermined by our behavior. First Peter 3:16 says, "Keep a good conscience so that in the thing in which you are slandered, those who revile your good behavior in Christ will be put to shame." This raises the possibility that one of the reasons for the ordered defense might be a slander about our behavior. "Keeping a good conscience" goes a long way in preventing slander and helps when we have to make a defense against it, if we have been unjustly slandered.

If you or I are guilty as charged, however, it undermines our credibility on other things. Thus the passage goes on to say, "For it is better, if God should will it so, that you suffer for doing what is right rather than for doing what is wrong" (1 Pet 3:17). If we have to suffer (v. 14), let us not be intimidated. Rather let us give a reasonable defense with gentleness and reverence, and keep a good conscience. In this way we will be suffering for righteousness' sake (see Mt 5:10-12) and not because we deserve it.

SUFFERING IN A GODLY MANNER IS A POWERFUL WITNESS

In the end, how we deal with suffering can be a powerful witness to the power of Christ. I think of a Chinese pastor whose church was taken away from him during the Cultural Revolution. He was forced to work in his former church building, which had been turned into a factory, for the next fifteen years. He was such a model of "gentleness and reverence" that his manner and his message spoke to all. Some of the guards were even moved to listen to him. After fifteen years, his church was restored to him and he ministered there for a number of years. When he died, people who had been touched by this man's life came from all over China.

His attitude of generosity in the face of suffering and evil was similar to that expressed by an anonymous soul in words found on brown wrapping paper at the Nazi concentration camp Ravensbrück:

> O Lord
> Remember not only the men and women of good will
> But also those of ill will
> But do not only remember the suffering they afflicted on us
> Remember the fruits we brought, thanks to this suffering.
> Our comradeship, our loyalty, our humility
> The courage, the generosity
> The greatness of heart, which has grown out of all this
> And when they come to judgment
> Let all the fruit that we have borne
> Be their forgiveness
> AMEN   AMEN   AMEN[7]

As a precondition for the effectiveness of our defense, we are called to not be intimidated. Instead, we are to sanctify Christ as Lord in our whole being, to respond with gentleness and reverence, to keep a good conscience and to suffer, if necessary, for righteousness' sake. In this manner, we can give a defense without being defensive.

PART 2

ARGUMENT AGAINST RELATIVISM

WHEN ARGUMENTS FAIL

Up to this point we have seen the importance of bending over backwards to point out that faith in Christ is not consistent with absolutism. This part will develop an argument against relativism. Today argument is not in fashion. However, argument has an important, if limited, place. Faith involves gaining *knowledge* of what the gospel is, giving *assent* to it and placing our *trust* in it. Moving people toward assent (which arguments can do) does not make somebody a believer, but it does help provide a necessary precondition for faith.

It has often been pointed out that unbelief is more a matter of the will than of the mind. Praying for the Holy Spirit's work is at least as important as presenting the gospel or arguing for it. Often people are more convinced by watching the practice of believers than by listening to any arguments put forth. C. S. Lewis said that "what we practice, not (save at rare intervals) what we preach is usually our great contribution to the conversion of others."[1] This does not mean that Lewis did not value argument. He often worked with evangelists such as Steven Olford, with Lewis addressing the audience for twenty minutes, clearing away obstacles to belief, and then Olford calling for commitment. It is difficult for the heart to embrace that which the mind rejects.

Having a rational justification for our position can be important for us, giving us confidence to speak to critics of the faith. This defense of the faith can also show that it is a lie to maintain that belief involves crucifying the mind or that believers cannot withstand the most difficult questions unbelievers can ask. This second part will provide a framework that will suggest a way of response to the often-raised issues about truth. While rarely will we be able to give a full case against relativism, it is still of value for us to know the case so that we can draw on whatever part we wish, like choosing the right golf club for a certain distance.

It is also important to underline the fact that many people may not be in the position to hear *any* arguments or we may have an open window for only a short time. In this chapter we will develop the importance of an indirect approach for closed people and then in later chapters develop a more direct argument against relativism that can be used where appropriate.

The truth is, each person is somewhere on the open-to-closed spectrum, and wisdom is needed to know how best to respond in each case. Here is a general rule to go by: the more open a person is, the more direct arguments can be used; the more closed a person is, the more an indirect approach is needed.[2] Only occasionally do we find a person who will share in a sustained discussion and follow it through to its end. In cases where a person is somewhat closed, an indirect approach using questions, stories, parables, riddles, short quotes or irony, or finding personal obstacles and discerning emotional sources of doubt, is necessary.

This chapter explores and illustrates how to take this less direct approach.

HYPOCRISY

Those who study cults have sometimes stated that cults are the "unpaid bills of the church." It is a sad truth, and the cults seem to capitalize particularly where the church has failed. Even the unbelief of many not involved with the cults can be attributed to the ills of the church and of individual Christians.

I have met many people who are reacting against Christianity or Christians, their greatest objection being that the "church is full of hypocrites," and they often relate painful incidences of such hypocrisy. In such cases empathy is the best response. In fact, if I say anything to these critics, I usually agree with their criticism. In addition, I like to use one small quote from G. K. Chesterton: "The best argument against Christianity is Christians." Sometimes this gets a laugh. Then I follow with the rest of the quote: "The best argument for Christianity is Christians." As one person commented, "I see. Just because *some* believers are bad examples, it does not mean *all* are bad examples." Another question is "Does the hypocrisy of some believers invalidate Christ?" And yet another: "Is their hypocrisy the *fruit* of faith in Christ or a *violation* of it?"

Given the opportunity, it is important to point out that there is a difference between a sinner and a hypocrite. All hypocrites are sinners, but not all sinners are hypocrites. Some sinners know they have done wrong and confess it. A hypocrite says one thing and does another; he or she sins and will not confess it. It is important to point out that people in the church are not "the good people," while those outside it are "the bad people." One writer said, "The church is much like Noah's Ark: if it weren't for the storm outside, you couldn't stand the smell inside." Those who believe in the gospel believe that each person needs to admit that he or she has sinned, then repent and trust in Christ alone for salvation. So it is to be hoped that people in the church know their sin and regularly admit it.

The very criticism of hypocrisy contains the moral judgment that hypocrisy is bad. When confronted with the charge of hypocrisy in the church, you might ask, "Where did you get the idea that hypocrisy is bad?" Might it be ultimately from Jesus, the strongest critic of the religious establishment on record? (See Matthew 23 and the seven "woes" Jesus pronounced on the religious leaders of his community.) The ultimate question is this: "Is Jesus a hypocrite, or is he who he says he is?"

Let me underscore my beginning point here: Before any of these observations can be made, it is important to listen and empathize with any real pain that hypocrisy has caused.

EMOTIONAL OBSTACLES
Many doubts are not rooted in intellectual issues at all. Of course, when

intellectual issues are raised, they need to be addressed. However, it is important to listen deeply for a significant amount of time to the questions being raised. I have often found that answering a question too quickly may cause me to miss the most important issue. It is better to say, "Tell me more," and listen for a while before responding.

Some time ago a Young Life leader referred a college student to me because the young man had recurring doubts about his faith. I met with the student a couple of times, talking not only about his intellectual questions but also about his life. In the end we mutually agreed that I had answered his intellectual objections. However, I cautioned him that our discussions may not have ended his doubts because I came to see that they were rooted in some deep emotional pain caused by many people, including his parents. These wounds made it difficult for him to trust and commit himself to anyone, including God, so I suggested that he go to a counselor in order to move toward healing. Happily, he agreed.

In fact, most of the doubts we encounter are emotional or spiritual in origin rather than intellectual. C. S. Lewis maintained,

> Supposing a man's reason once decides that the weight of evidence is for it [the gospel claim]. I can tell that man what is going to happen to him in the next few weeks. . . . There will come a moment when he wants a woman, or wants to tell a lie, or feels very pleased with himself, or sees a chance of making a little money in some way that is not perfectly fair; some moment at which it would be convenient if Christianity were not true. And his emotions will carry out a blitz. I am not talking of any moments at which any real reasons against Christianity turn up. Those have to be faced, and that is a different matter. I am talking about moments where a mere mood rises up against it. . . . Now faith in the sense in which I am here using the word is the art of holding onto the things your reason has once accepted, in spite of your changing moods. For moods change whatever view your reason takes.[3]

The emotional issues must be addressed before a passionate commitment to truth in Christ can be sustained.

EDUCATION IS IMPLICATION

G. K. Chesterton once said, "Education is implication." What we remember from the books we read and the teachers we hear are mostly things that were between the lines or implied in what was said. Perhaps we remember a few specific quotes, but often we express—perhaps in different words—those impressions given us from the reigning passions of our teachers.

I was once discussing the issue of teaching religion and ethics in the public schools with the education department chairperson at a Christian college. Since he often served as a consultant and visited many public schools, he made a couple of observations. First, he had discovered the top teachers in each school were often believers in Christ. Second, he had discerned that, even though the Christian teachers could rarely if ever speak explicitly about their faith or values in the school, their belief shone through anyway. He said, "The teacher is the moral value." As long as believers teach in public schools, their values will be communicated one way or another. The classic way of putting this is to say that education and morality are "caught" as well as "taught."

Of course, this can work in the other direction too. If the teacher habitually omits God from any consideration, or gives a caustic remark when religion is mentioned, this will also be communicated to the student. Many students all through school, particularly in high school, college and graduate school, are in environments where relativism of many shades (including postmodernism) is rampant. Often students are swayed to this perspective not by the arguments given in support of these views but because of the constant stream of implicit relativism the students have encountered throughout the year. Believers often are influenced by the environment in which they study.

It is important to keep this phenomenon in mind when talking to a relativist. It takes more than a few arguments to change a whole manner of thinking. If a water channel has been covered over with silt, it needs to be dredged before it can be used again. If the impact of relativism has been at the levels of reason, emotion and imagination, then the antidote needs to be more than rational. It is important to take the time to show people in their experience, practice and rationality the implications of believing in Christ. Postmodernism is sometimes described as a mood of suspicion. The deeper the inbred suspicion, the more difficult it is to shake.

USING QUESTIONS

Sometimes a question goes deeper into the heart than an answer. Jesus was a master of asking questions. He often did not give a direct answer to questions asked of him, because he wanted to probe more deeply into what lay behind the question.

For instance, the rich young ruler came to Jesus asking him the question "Good Teacher, what shall I do to inherit eternal life?" Jesus responded to this question with a question: "Why do you call Me good? No one is good except God alone." Jesus went on to quote the commandments from the "second table" of the Ten Commandments, the fifth through tenth. The ruler's response was "All these things I have kept from my youth." Seeing that the young man had a superficial idea of goodness, Jesus responded, "One thing you still lack; sell all that you possess and distribute it to the poor, and you shall have treasure in heaven; and come, follow Me" (Lk 18:18-22). Jesus zeroed in on the young man's problem: his god was his riches. He was, in effect, violating the first commandment, "You shall have no other gods before Me." Again notice how the use of a question to respond to a question allowed Jesus to go deeper than giving a theoretical theological answer. His response showed that even the question was wrong and that "doing" to "inherit eternal life" was a wrong way of stating things.

Jesus particularly used questions with closed people. For instance, the prologue to the Good Samaritan story (Lk 10:25-37) begins with a question. A lawyer asked Jesus, "Teacher, what shall I do to inherit eternal life?" (v. 25). Jesus responded not with an answer but with a question: "What is written in the Law? How does it read to you?" (v. 26). The lawyer proceeded to give the Great Commandment just as Jesus had done elsewhere (see Mt 22:37-39). Jesus' response was "Do this and you will live" (Lk 10:28). The lawyer, perhaps having planned this question all along, asked, "And who is my neighbor?" (v. 29)—a raging debate in rabbinic circles. Jesus told the parable of the Good Samaritan, ending with a question: "Which of these three do you think proved to be a neighbor to the man who fell into the robber's hands?" (v. 36). The lawyer's answer was "The one [notice that the lawyer seems unable to even say the word Samaritan] who showed mercy toward him." Jesus' response was "Go and do the same" (v. 37).

Notice here that the lawyer asked two questions, and each time Jesus responded with another question. Each time the lawyer came up with the right answer himself, and Jesus only had to confirm it and call him to live accordingly. Clearly this lawyer was not coming to have a friendly chat; rather he was coming to put Jesus to the test (v. 25). The lawyer evidently wished to "justify himself" (v. 29), but Jesus' questions evoked right answers from the lawyer, allowing him to see himself as in a mirror.

We find many other instances like this in Scripture. Suffice it to say that wisdom dictates whether it is good to give a direct answer to a question. A rule of thumb: The more closed and hostile the person is, the more a direct answer would be futile—and the more likely a question may rattle around in their brain longer than an answer.

USING QUOTES

Often I have found that short quotes are more effective than long answers, especially when we are talking to closed people. First of all, we may not get the time for a long discussion because of a limited window of opportunity or limited openness. Most people will not sit still long enough for a half-hour or hour presentation, so the open window may be only seconds in duration.

Once I was meeting with a top international leader of the New Age movement who is a published author and much in demand on the speaking circuit. She was very open to discussing the person of Jesus, but when I raised a question from one of her books that denied the reality of sin and evil, we found a point of deep disagreement. I used this Chesterton quote: "People have given up on the idea of original sin when it's the only doctrine of Christianity that can be empirically proven." She laughed, and I knew it had registered. We also found another point of contact in a book we had both read, *People of the Lie* by Scott Peck. As we discussed his idea that sin is "life taking" and some of the stories contained in the book, I could see she was wrestling with this idea. I happened to call her four months later, and her first comment to me was "I've been thinking about that idea of sin for the past four months!" Yet she did not have any answers.

Another quotation that has proved helpful is the old proverb "An argument against abuse is not an argument against use." Often people uncritically equate the abuse of faith with the true article. This quote puts the issue clearly and concisely.

As you can see, it is good to develop a number of short, concise, pithy ways of saying things. This is consistent with Scripture's word that our speech is to be full of grace and seasoned with salt (Col 4:6).

PERSONAL ANALOGY

Sometimes the best means of getting through to a relativist is to use a personal analogy, something that the other person can easily grasp because it is already a part of his or her life. Of course, the particular nature of the analogy will depend upon the person.

Chuck Colson tells the story of a time on a talk show when he mentioned the word *absolutes*. After the show the nationally known interviewer teased Colson about his use of the term. This led to a lengthy discussion of the issue in a back room. After all of Colson's arguments proved futile, he found a personal point of contact. Knowing the man's way of life, he asked, "You like to sail, don't you?"

Interviewer: "Yes."

Colson: "Can you sail at night?"

Interviewer: "Yes."

Colson: "How can you sail at night, when you can't see?"

Interviewer: "Well, I use the stars."

Colson: "How can you use the stars?"

Interviewer: "Because, they are fixed points. Oh, I see what you are saying: we need some fixed points by which we can orient ourselves."[4]

In this case a personal analogy helped where the term *absolute* might have been an obstacle.

Sometimes knowledge of what a person loves can lead to an effective analogy to use in the discussion because people often think most about that which they love. Often the point of contact can be a favorite book, movie, music group, song or sport. These areas can provide creative ways to make connections with spiritual struggles and questions.

DOGMA IS DRAMA

Stories can also provide a good way to connect with people. My experience in giving talks over the years has shown me which stories people remember. They tend to remember those stories that have been made most vivid to their senses. Perhaps the story we need to tell best is the gospel.

Dorothy Sayers, a friend of C. S. Lewis and J. R. R. Tolkien, was an Oxford-educated writer of detective stories, dramas and religious essays. In one such essay, "The Greatest Drama Ever Staged," she argued that the problem of dullness in the church is not because of dogma but because of the lack of it. The gospel story, she said, is "the tale of the time when God was the underdog and got beaten when he submitted to the conditions he had laid down and became a man like men he had made, and the men he had made broke him and killed him."

> This is the dogma we find so dull—this terrifying drama of which God is the victim and hero. . . . If this is dull, then what, in heaven's name, is worthy to be called exciting? . . . The people who hanged Christ never, to do them justice, accused him of being a bore. On the contrary, they thought him too dynamic to be safe. It has been left for later generations to muffle up that shattering personality and surround him with an atmosphere of tedium. We have very efficiently pared the claws of the Lion of Judah, certified him meek and mild and recommended him as a fitting household pet for pale curates and old ladies.[5]

At the end of the essay, Sayers wrote,

> Now we may call that doctrine exhilarating, or we may call it devastating; we may call it revelation, or we may call it rubbish; but if we call it dull, then words can have no meaning at all. That God should play the tyrant over man is a dismal story of unrelieved oppression; that man should play tyrant over man is the usual dreary record of human futility; but that man should play the tyrant over God and find him a better man than he is an astonishing drama indeed. Any journalist, hearing of it for the first time, would recognize it as news; those who did hear it for the first time actually called it news, and good news at that; though we are likely to forget that the word Gospel ever meant anything so sensational.[6]

In another essay, "The Dogma Is the Drama," Sayers followed a similar theme. She was once in a discussion about her play *The Zeal of Thy House,* which dramatizes Christian doctrines. The questioners were astonished at the content of the play, thinking that she must have made it up. She insisted, "If the play were dramatic, it was so, not in spite of the dogma, but because of it—that in short, the dogma is the drama."[7] The questioners had a difficult time believing it. She finished her essay with another bold statement.

> It is the dogma that is the drama—not beautiful phrases, nor comforting sentiments, nor vague aspirations to loving-kindness and uplift, nor the promise of something nice after death—but the terrifying assertion that the same God who made the world, lived in the world and passed through the grave and gate of death. Show that to the heathen, and they may not believe it; but at least they may realize that here is something that a man might be glad to believe.[8]

The apostle Paul said, "You foolish Galatians, who has bewitched you, before whose eyes Jesus Christ was publicly portrayed as crucified?" (Gal 3:1). The word for "publicly portrayed" carries the sense of being placarded or painted in front of others like a billboard. Does this imply that Paul's practice and that of the early church was to vividly portray the gospel story in pictorial language? Perhaps so. There is certainly much drama in the gospel stories. We do not have to add drama to the text; it is already there. The first stories we need to learn to tell are those about Jesus. There is much drama in the dogma.

IMAGINATION

A poll of *Christianity Today* readers found that, other than the Bible, the one book that has most influenced their lives was C. S. Lewis's *Mere Christianity*. Lewis's popularity shows no sign of waning; if anything, it is increasing. What is the key to his continuing impact? An essential part of the answer would be the way in which he combined reason and imagination.

Other authors who have been considered culture shapers have, like Lewis, employed more than one form of literature to communicate. Jean-Paul Sartre (1905–1980), for instance, could write philosophy (*Being and Nothingness*) as well as drama (*No Exit*). In other words, his ideas were communicated in rational discourse and via the imagination by means of drama. Similarly, C. S. Lewis could give an argument against relativism in his nonfiction work *The Abolition of Man* or effectively counter it in his novel *That Hideous Strength.*

Lewis argued at one point that, while reason is the natural organ of truth, "imagination is the organ of meaning." In other words, we do not really grasp the meaning of a word or concept until we have a clear image with which we can connect it. You can find a more detailed argument of this contention in *Selected Literary Essays* (see "Bluspels and Flalansferes").[9] The practical effect of this belief in Lewis's writing was that, even in the midst of an apologetic argument, he provided just the right picture, image or metaphor to help the reader grasp the meaning of the argument. For instance, note his use of image and analogy in this quote from *The Weight of Glory:*

> Our Lord finds our desires not too strong, but too weak. We are half-hearted creatures, fooling about with drink, sex, and ambition when infinite joy is offered us, like an ignorant child who wants to go on making mud pies in a slum because he cannot imagine what is meant by the offer of a holiday at the sea. We are far too easily pleased.[10]

The "mud pies" and "the holiday at the sea" help us glimpse what it means to be "far too easily pleased" or to impoverish our own desires.

Most of Lewis's major ideas are also developed in his fiction. Similarly, if we are going to communicate truth powerfully, we need to use the "organ of meaning" (imagination) as well as the "organ of truth" (reason).

It is not surprising that Lewis used imagination well in his apologetic writings, for imagination played a key role in Lewis's conversion. Once in a bookstore he bought a copy of George MacDonald's *Phantastes.* As he read it, a "new quality" touched Lewis's life. He first described this quality as a "bright shadow" but later came to realize it was "holiness." In recalling the night after reading *Phantastes,* Lewis said that his imagination was "baptized," although "the rest of me, not unnaturally took longer."[11]

Lewis also held a number of rational objections to faith. One by one, though, his arguments against the faith were answered until, already having his imagination "baptized" and his reason satisfied, he felt the "steady, unrelenting approach of Him whom I so earnestly desired not to meet." Finally he gave in, knelt and prayed one night, "the most dejected and reluctant convert in all England."[12] His conversion fits the pattern shown in figure 8.1.

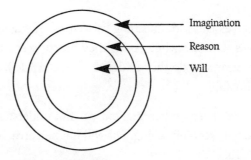

Figure 8.1. The conversion pattern of C. S. Lewis

First, his imagination was "baptized." Then his reason was satisfied. Then he submitted his will. Having his imagination baptized did not take him all the way to faith, but it was an important first step. In a similar manner, telling stories or reading good books together with unbelievers may provide an avenue for further discussion. The organ of meaning can point to the organ of truth.

Once I was teaching a class on C. S. Lewis's apologetics for Young Life in Colorado. A young atheist was visiting from out of town and was invited to come to the class. She had just read Lewis's novel *The Lion, the Witch and the Wardrobe* but had no idea that the novel had anything to do with Christ. Our discussions over lunch those couple of days proved very productive. This same approach can apply to works written by nonbelievers as well. Often these contain brilliant observations that point to deep human aspirations that can only be adequately grounded in a belief in God and his Son, Jesus. In this way imagination and stories can be important tools for pre-evangelism.

PARABLES

Jesus often used parables, not to provide us with nice stories to act out in Sunday school but as weapons in controversy. Remember, the disciples and others did not immediately understand the parables (see Mt 13:18-23). The meaning of the parables was clear only if one "had eyes to see."

Parables can hide meaning as well as enlighten. Jesus said he used parables "because while seeing they do not see, and while hearing they do not hear, nor do they understand" (Mt 13:13). He went on to quote from Isaiah,

> You will keep on hearing, but will not understand;
> You will keep on seeing, but will not perceive.
> (Mt 13:14; see Is 6:9)

People can hear and yet not really hear, see and yet not really see.

Parables are an indirect form of teaching that may possibly be subversive or squeeze through a crack in someone's hardened heart. It is particularly used and sometimes effective with closed people. For instance, recall the parable that the prophet Nathan told King David about a rich man who owned many sheep and a poor man who owned only one sheep (2 Sam 12:1-4). To feed a visiting guest, the rich man took the poor man's only sheep rather than one of his many. King David, not knowing it was a parable, was outraged and declared that this rich man deserved to die. Nathan, seeing his opening, proclaimed, "You are the man!" (v. 7). David replied, "I have sinned against the LORD" (v. 13). If Nathan had directly confronted David with his sin, who knows what may have happened? David may have killed Nathan in a burst of anger. Yet at the moment David was in hot indignation against the injustice of the rich man's theft, he was most open to see what he had taken—Uriah's life and his wife.

Another illustration would be the parable of the prodigal son (more properly titled "the parable of the two lost sons"). The prodigal son is such a great story that we forget that it was told to Pharisees and scribes who were upset with how Jesus "receives sinners and eats with them" (Lk 15:2). Jesus not only remained in a room when sinners arrived, but he also "received" them, perhaps even inviting them to dinner—an intimate form of fellowship in Jewish culture. Jesus proceeded to tell the offended Pharisees the parables of the lost sheep, the lost coin and the two lost sons. Interestingly, he left the second part of the last parable unfinished. Will the elder son come into the party and rejoice in his wayward brother's return, or will he stay forever outside in his self-pity and sense of superiority? Jesus' accusers were forced to see themselves in the mirror of this story. Which were they: like the merciful father of the parable or like the elder son? If they were not moved to repentance, they must have walked away frustrated and angry at this accurate depiction of their own attitudes. If they had eyes to see, ears to hear and hearts to feel, this parable could enable them to change their attitudes toward tax collectors and sinners (v. 1).

Many of Jesus' forty-one parables (depending on how you count them) fall in this category: they were spoken to closed people who were given the opportunity to see or not see, hear or not hear. We can use Jesus' parables or modern parables, or even make up our own parable, to speak to closed people stuck in their unbelief.

IRONY

One indirect approach that can sometimes be successful (but that is not for the faint in heart) is irony. Its purpose, like that of the parable, is to turn the mirror on the audience, so they can see themselves starkly. Writing in a Catholic magazine, Michael Novak said,

> At many private dinners these days, when the conversation sooner or later turns to abortion, contraception, gay rights, women priests, or any one of the many other sex and gender issues that in-

flame the passions of our time, the Catholics present may sooner or later be turned upon. A friend reports that at such dinners, when he may be the only Catholic present, he adopts an ironic mode of response. It always works, he says, to bring to light a desperate longing among modern people to be told that their own current passions are mistaken and destructive.

If my friend's dinner interlocutors accuse the Church of backwardness, he agrees, even asserting that the Catholic church should begin to teach young children that there are no sexual sins; that everything is permitted and that their Christian duty is free experimentation into every nook and cranny of sexual possibility. All this he says very quietly, as if without irony, and in a calm and ecumenical tone. (When a devilish spirit arises in his breast, however, he sometimes adds quietly: "Woody Allen understands natural law better than the Pope does: 'What the heart wants, the heart wants.'")

When my friend is finished speaking, there is dead silence. It is not the route his dinner companions want the Catholic Church to take. If it did, who would be left to hold the line, any line, for their children?

My friend's conclusion is the following: "What your fellow guests actually want is for you to defend in public what they will not. They want the pleasant feeling of being more progressive than thou, while having you defend what they do not dare to defend (but absolutely count on). That is a pleasure you must never ever allow them to indulge."[13]

It takes courage and dramatic flair to use irony well, but as you can see, it can be quite effective.

LOVE

Above all, we need to practice love. Love is the most attractive of virtues and is to be the mark of the believer. Christ's love is distinctive and sets us apart from adherents of other religions and worldviews.

Many New Age people are very loving and sensitive to the world and others around them. But this is not always the case. I once spent a few hours with a senior researcher at a large New Age think tank, where he had been working full time for fifteen years. He confided that he had never found a "home" in any of the Eastern views. Now after fifteen years of deep immersion in the New Age, he was considering returning to the Jesus of his youth. The reason for his growing dissatisfaction emerged when he commented that he had met all the leading gurus and top New Age leaders, and he was profoundly disappointed, finding them "very narcissistic." I pointed out to him that, although many New Age people do not live consistently with this, the whole thrust of the New Age is *inward*, to "the god within," or *upward*, to merge one's identity with that of the One. But it is definitely not *outward*, because the world is somehow either "illusory" or "nondistinct." The more consistently you try to live out this philosophy, the less you are thrust out to love real people. He agreed that this was the case.

Tal Brooke, now president of Spiritual Counterfeits Project in Berkeley, California, was for some years a disciple of India's guru of gurus, Sai Baba. In fact, he was being groomed to be a Western spokesman for the guru, and he had a number of private audiences with him. This special attention was very unusual. Sai Baba is considered by many to be the leading guru in India. Many other gurus go to him to be blessed. Many Hindus, and many in the New Age movement, travel a long way to catch a glimpse of him.

Tal met a Christian missionary couple while in India and set out to convert them to Hinduism by the sheer force of his intellect. They intellectually addressed some of his criticisms, but what made the biggest impact on him was the quality of their love for him. It was what he came later to describe as an other-centered, agape love, because it seemed to him that they loved him more than they loved or cared for themselves. He noted that although there was a gentleness in the Hindu disciples around him, they lacked this other-centered love. Above all, the guru of gurus, Sai Baba, was utterly lacking in this agape love. As I heard Tal describe this over dinner, I got goose bumps, recalling Jesus' statement in John 13:35: "By this all men will know that you are My disciples, if you have love for one another."

Secular relativism and postmodernism also lack this outward thrust and philosophically push their adherents in an inward direction. Their teachings state that either you or your community makes up your values; there is no necessary thrust outside you. Again, many people hold to these views yet live inconsistently with them. The point I am making is that there is nothing in these views that philosophically necessitates your getting outside yourself to love others.

The love of Christ may in fact be the ultimate apologetic. This was powerfully demonstrated to me during a conference in which evangelical leaders and top New Age leaders were invited to focus on the person of Jesus. As a part of the conference, many people shared their spiritual journeys. Not surprisingly, Christians and Christianity had profoundly hurt many of the New Age leaders. The collective heart of the evangelical leaders sank as we heard story after story of pain caused by Christians. At one point Bob Mitchell (at that time president of Young Life) apologized, with tears, to the New Age leaders on behalf of all the believers present. It was a moving moment.

At the end of the conference, one of the women who was the wife of a top New Age leader shared that these days had an immense impact on her. Because of what some Christians had done to her fifteen years ago, she had not been able even to say the name of Jesus Christ. As she said that name, she broke down and wept uncontrollably. I left that time more in love with Jesus than ever before.

Always we must remember what Jesus said: "I, if I am lifted up from the earth, will draw all men to Myself" (Jn 12:32).

ABSOLUTISTS IN DISGUISE?

BILL: *So, what is your case against relativism?*

JOHN: *I suppose it could be summed up like this: relativism has severe problems both logically and practically. If a position is held, it should be able to be thought and lived. I find problems in both areas. Let's start with practical inconsistency. I have yet to meet or read a relativist who is not an absolutist in disguise.*

༄

Have you noticed a curious fact? Many relativists are really absolutists. For instance, many maintain a radical relativism that forbids us to judge another culture, yet they often stand (rightly) against the oppression of women and racism in our own culture. But if we do not have a sufficient basis to judge another culture, how do we have a sufficient basis to judge our own?

An illustration of this dilemma is found in David Lehman's book *Signs of the Times: Deconstructionism and the Fall of Paul de Man.* This book is a fascinating account of how the radically relativistic philosophy of deconstructionism has attempted to come to terms with the fact that one of the movement's founders, Paul de Man (1919–1983), wrote a number of anti-Semitic articles for a Nazi-sympathizing newspaper. Many of the relativists in the academic world hate anti-Semitism, yet their philosophy provides no "neutral ground" on which to condemn it. The second half of Lehman's book shows how many postmodernists turn themselves into pretzels rather than admit the obvious.

Charles Griswold of Howard University commented,

Is there anything in Deconstructionism that could serve as a basis for repudiating (and providing an ethical critique of) Nazism? Granted for the moment that the theory does not logically entail Nazism, and lots of perfectly acceptable people have taken a shine to the theory. Does the theory provide a basis for criticism of that sort of political program? I doubt that it does, and this because it renders theoretically unintelligible basic moral terms, such as "good" and "evil." . . . De Man's theory does not permit us to utter the sentence "Nazism is evil" with any theoretical justification. When pressed, we could only say that given the sensibility of one's empirical state at the moment the statement was uttered, it is felt that Nazism is evil (or good as the case may be). Is not an account to that effect morally suspect?[1]

INCONSISTENCY

Despite the lack of justification or adequate grounding for their moral views, many relativists wax eloquent on many moral and social causes. Jean-François Lyotard, the French philosopher, defined postmodernism as "incredulity toward metanarratives," or a suspicion of any all-encompassing stories because such perspectives have been oppressive. For instance, Nazism and Marxism give a comprehensive account of the world and both have been extremely oppressive. Christianity provides a comprehensive story that proceeds from eternity to creation, fall, redemption and consummation, thus making it a metanarrative of which postmodernists like Lyotard are highly suspicious. Unquestionably, there have been times when the church has been unjust and oppressive, as during the Inquisition and the Crusades. But do all metanarratives lead to oppression as the postmodernists suggest? (Note that a judgment is made: oppression is believed to be evil or wrong.) Oppression and injustice are indeed bad. On what grounds, however, can a postmodernist assume that oppression and injustice are objectively evil? Postmodernism is a deeply moral critique of the dangers of absolutism, yet it lacks an absolute standard of justice with which to make that critique.

Jacques Derrida (b. 1930), one of the founders of postmodernism, calls for deconstructing narratives in order to see the tensions and contradictions in each text. The only exemption from deconstruction is deconstructionism itself. The reason? Because "Deconstruction is Justice."[2] No reason is given, however, as to why deconstruction is exempt or what justice involves.

Many relativists write books attempting to persuade others of their views or attempting to describe a better way for society. They have a sense of purpose and passion about their contribution to society. Unlike Derrida's bold stance, many do not make themselves exempt from criticism, yet there is a profound tension and self-refuting quality to their views.

Sooner or later all positions of this kind will make some kind of judgment about what is good for the educational system, the nation or the world. Perhaps they will not use the word *good* but another substituted term. In *The Abolition of Man,* Lewis argued,

> To abstain from calling it "good" and to use such predicates as "necessary", "progressive", or "efficient" would be a subterfuge. They could be forced in debate to answer the questions "necessary for what?" or "progressing towards what?" or "effecting what?" In the last resort they would have to admit that some state of affairs is good for its own sake: . . . Their skepticism about values is on the surface: it is for other people's values, and about the values current in their own set; they are not nearly skeptical enough. A great many of those who "debunk" traditional or (as they would say) sentimental values have in the background values of their own which they believe to be immune from the debunking process.[3]

TAKING THE ROOF OFF

When Francis Schaeffer first founded the Swiss meeting place L' Abri for intellectuals, a friend of mine went to visit. An atheist, he held to relativism as a philosophy but was passionate about injustice. At that time he was upset about the Vietnam War and other American abuses. In discussion it was pointed out that he could not both have the freedom of relativism to do whatever he wanted in his personal life and also have an absolute standard by which he could condemn injustice. Why was he so certain that there was justice or injustice if there was no God? He was provoked to make a choice: become a consistent relativist or accept an adequate basis for justice in a God who is there and is not silent on moral issues. He finally chose belief in God through Christ.

Francis Schaeffer's approach is still valuable today. He stressed the importance of "taking the roof off," that is, exposing the tensions and contradictions of unbelief. In a sense Schaeffer deconstructed before deconstructionism. In his book *The God Who Is There*, Schaeffer mentioned an interchange with a young Hindu at Cambridge who was speaking strongly against Christianity. Schaeffer countered by pointing out the problems in Hinduism: "Am I not correct in saying that, on the basis of your system, cruelty and noncruelty are ultimately equal, that there is no intrinsic difference between them?" The young Hindu agreed that this was the case. At this point the student in whose room they were meeting picked up a steaming teapot and stood with it over the young Hindu man's head as if to pour it on him. Alarmed, the young man asked what the student was doing. The student responded, "Cruelty is the same as non-cruelty," thus effectively bringing home the tension between theory and practice.[4]

Similarly, while I was briefly interim pastor for the First Congregational Church in Woodstock, Vermont, I met a young man in a coffee shop who was beginning to believe in reincarnation. We had a few lengthy conversations over the next several weeks, and one of the points that most impressed him was that reincarnation was based on the inflexible system of good and bad karma. Where was there any basis for forgiveness, mercy and grace? He was a very relational and outgoing young man who wanted to be married and have children. He began to see the philosophical relationship between reincarnation and what he wanted, producing profound tension between his highest aspirations and what he was coming to believe. On the other hand, I showed him how faith in Christ thrusts one out to love, value relationship, willingly forgive and care for each person's value. In this instance what I did was to push him toward an adequate basis for his highest aspirations.

Why Reorganize Illusion?

New Age spirituality is Eastern religion in Western dress. Although New Agers hold a bewildering number of viewpoints on secondary matters, they share some foundational beliefs. It is similar to a beef stew. Everybody knows what a beef stew is like. But just because you have had one beef stew, it does not mean you have had them all. Cooks put in different cuts of beef, different vegetables and different spices. Likewise, New Age spirituality draws from various Eastern religious traditions, such as Hinduism, Buddhism and Taoism, and it may also include Native American and shamanistic practices. When you add various elements of Christianity, Islam and spirit channeling, the possible combinations are many. Every practitioner creates his or her own unique mix. But what is the common ground that makes it New Age? The central principles held in common are the following:

1. All is one.
2. You are god.
3. Altered consciousness is the goal.
4. Unlimited power is available.

The all-is-one belief could also be stated in a negative fashion as the principle of nondistinction. In other words, New Age believers hold to some form of pantheism (all is God) or monism (there is only one being). The related but secondary principle is that you are god or participate in divinity. If all is god and you are part of the all, then you are a part of god. Third, the purpose of life is to alter consciousness so that you see that all is one and you are divine. This is where numerous methodologies, including holistic health techniques, are used. Some have dubbed these methods of altering consciousness "psychotechnologies." Fourth, the New Age offers a promise of unlimited power. Since you in a sense create your own reality, then anything is possible if you alter your consciousness. Advocates emphasize different aspects of these four principles, usually the "psychotechnologies" or unlimited power, but sooner or later the "all is one" and "you are god" beliefs surface.

Recent popularizers of this spirituality have found creative ways to articulate the all-is-one philosophy. For instance, Deepak Chopra said toward the beginning of his bestseller *The Seven Spiritual Laws of Success,* "The physical universe is nothing other than the Self curving back within Itself to experience Itself."[5] In the same context he said that there are "seeds of divinity within us" and that we are "divinity in disguise."[6] In Chopra's book *Ageless Body, Timeless Mind,* he agreed with an Indian teacher who said:

As is the microcosm, so is the macrocosm.
As is the atom, so is the universe.
As is the human body, so is the cosmic body.
As is the human mind, so is the cosmic mind.[7]

Andrew Weil has emerged in the alternative medicine field and, after years of obscurity, made the cover of *Time* magazine (May 12, 1997). He also echoes this all-is-one perspective. He said in *Natural Health, Natural Medicine,* "All religions and spiritual traditions stress the importance of overcoming the illusion of separateness and experiencing unity."[8] Weil, like Chopra, was educated in medicine and applies his philosophy to issues of health.

Gary Zukav, who like Chopra was given extensive national publicity by appearing on the *Oprah* television show, also holds to the belief that all is one. In his popular book *The Seat of the Soul,* he said, "Physical reality and the organisms and forms within physical reality are systems of Light within systems of light, and this Light is the same Light as the Light of your soul."[9] The ancient Hindu way of saying the same thing is "Atman is Brahman"—the individual is one with the divine.

Both Zukav and Chopra use the Hindu metaphor of a drop being absorbed in the ocean. Our destiny, in other words, is loss of our individuality in the great ocean of being—the One. Zukav said,

> You have always been because what it is that you are is God or Divine intelligence, but God takes on individual forms, droplets, reducing its power to small particles of individual consciousness. . . . As the little form grows in power, in self-hood, in its own consciousness of the self, it becomes larger and more Godlike. The it becomes God.[10]

In a similar way Chopra said that our destiny is to merge or be absorbed into the One. He said in his videotaped series *Return of the Wizard,* "The drop becomes the ocean and the ocean becomes the drop. The cosmos is one's body."[11]

The all-is-one philosophy also leads to the conclusion that there is no distinction between good and evil. Gary Zukav said, "When we say of an action, 'This is right' or 'That is wrong,' we create negative karma."[12] Consider what he is saying: there is no right and no wrong, but there is a distinction between negative and positive karma. Is not negative karma wrong? By what standards do we know what is negative and positive?

I believe that there is a contradiction between the all-is-one philosophy (nondistinction) and the role of karma. If all distinctions are illusory, is not also the distinction between negative and positive karma illusory? If it is illusory, why do we need to take it seriously? Is not negative karma "wrong" in disguise? One author pointed out that the more philosophical the advocate of monism (all is one), the less emphasis is placed on karma and reincarnation because of the tensions involved. In any case, note Zukav's denial that we can say that there is anything "right" or "wrong."

SELECTIVE MORALITY

The New Age principle of nondistinction poses great difficulty for the practical need to live in reality and make moral decisions. The affirmation of nondistinction leads to the loss of a real distinction between true and false as well as between good and evil.

New Age writer Marilyn Ferguson, in her influential book *The Aquarian Conspiracy,* subtitled her vision "Personal and Social Transformation in the 1980s." She proceeded to outline great agendas for the emergence of the individual into a state of near godhood and the emergence of a great and just society. However, Ferguson never seemed to notice that there is a marked tension between an aspiration of personal transformation and the ultimate destiny of absorption and extinction maintained by some forms of Hinduism and Buddhism. One has to ask, what kind of personal transformation leads to the loss of personality? And in the social arena, formulating a plan for every area of life as she does must of necessity involve many complex distinctions. But why on the basis of the New Age view of reality as illusory would you want to reorganize "illusion"? Furthermore, how could your plan make the world "better" if there is no good and evil?

Ferguson herself pointed out the implications of nondistinction, noting that spiritual traditions holding to this view of reality maintain "there is no good or evil."[13] Ferguson even quoted the example of a young therapist who, on seeing that separations and distinctions are unreal, came to the conclusion "that I am already whole, that there is nothing to overcome. In those moments of emptiness, of letting be, of complete contact with another, I know that I am all I can be."[14] The only sin, it seems, is ignorance of wholeness and unity; the only evil is the belief in separation or distinction. There is no basis for guilt in the New Age perspective because there is no fixed standard by which one can be judged.

Of course it is difficult, if not impossible, to speak to social issues without making moral judgments. For instance, Ferguson's chapter on politics is entitled "Right Power." Immediately this title implies that there is a wrong kind of power. In another section she suggested, "In this wholeness, oddly enough, virtues we might once have sought in vain through moral concepts now come spontaneously."[15] Here the use of the term "virtues" implies the existence of vices.

In the area of education Ferguson critiqued the old academic (left brain) way of education. She is in favor of an approach that is more creative (right brain), taking into account altered states of consciousness. Ferguson supports a curriculum that takes altered states of consciousness seriously and advocates the use of "centering," meditation and other exercises that would encourage "whole brain learning."[16]

In the area of vocation Ferguson calls for a redefinition of security and success. Above all she calls people to "go for it," moving out of conventional jobs and into ones corresponding to their dreams and desires. Follow the way that makes you feel better and enhances consciousness; reject that which dulls consciousness, such as repetitive, conventional jobs.

In the area of medicine she critiques those who fail to take into account the whole person. She argues for holistic health practices.

While believers would certainly agree with some of Ferguson's social critique (although for very different reasons), it must be pointed out that none of Ferguson's critiques are consistent with the principle of nondistinction. Ferguson makes many distinctions, moral and otherwise, but she makes them selectively. Often New Age advocates employ Western science, logic, literary style and morality when it is to their advantage. When it is not, they shout, "Western rationalist!" Ferguson seems to be unaware of the influence of moral values and assumptions in her use of language, logical distinctions, moral judgments and social critique.

Not long ago I asked one New Age advocate how he could make so many prescriptions for society when all is one and there is no basis for the distinction between good and evil. He said that moral distinctions are necessary because we live in this illusory world and that is just the way it is now. I asked him, "If the One is beyond good and evil, why should I take morality seriously now, because it is illusory?" He admitted that he did not know how to answer this question.

NEOPAGAN TENSIONS

Neopaganism—the new witchcraft, also known as Wicca or the Craft—

is a new and growing movement in America. Some have suggested that it is the fastest-growing religion in America. While its numbers may not yet be large, its impact on college campuses, in theological seminaries and in radical feminism is significant. Wicca claims to be a return to an ancient nature religion often centered on the worship of Mother Earth and the moon goddess Diana or other goddesses. Neopagans use ancient rites and rituals such as "drawing down the moon," or they create their own rites that are practiced at the full moon—outside in the open air and "sky clad" (naked). This is a complex religious movement with no hierarchy, and each coven is essentially autonomous. There are, however, certain points of agreement among them.

Neopagans, like New Agers, deny any absolute distinction between good and evil—and for a similar reason: they believe that all is one (although this is not always clearly articulated). In fact, neopagans hold to all four assumptions of the New Age spirituality, except with a different emphasis. Neopagans put the emphasis on unlimited power (principle 4) available to alter reality. That reality is changed by altering consciousness (principle 3) through rite and ritual, and it is supposed to work because we are divine (principle 2) and all is one (principle 1). In neopagan author Margot Adler's influential book *Drawing Down the Moon* (which defines the unity behind the diversity in the new witchcraft), she said, "Many people said they had become pagans because they could be themselves and act as they chose without what they felt were medieval notions of sin and guilt."[17] Later Adler summarized, "Neo-pagans embrace the values of spontaneity, nonauthoritarianism, anarchism, pluralism, polytheism, animism, sensuality, passion, a belief in the goodness of pleasure."[18]

Neopaganism's polytheism is not an emphasis on there being many distinct gods but a return to animism and pantheism (all is one). Adler commented on the relationship between pantheism and the deity of each neopagan:

> For many pagans, pantheism implies much the same thing as animism. It is a view that divinity is inseparable from nature and that

deity is immanent in nature. Neo-pagan groups participate in divinity. . . . This idea was well expressed in the quotation at the beginning of the *Whole Earth Catalog:* "We are gods and might as well get good at it." The Neo-Pagan Church of All Worlds has expressed this idea by the phrase "Thou Art God/dess."[19]

Philip Davis, in his account of the emergence of neopaganism, pointed out that in the goddess movement this relativistic "denial of the transcendent essentially eliminates any foundation for absolute moral standards."[20] Davis later showed the consequences of this denial of absolutes: "In the goddess movement, consequently, the neo-pagan rejection of moral limits is most fully articulated in the realm of sex."[21] (See below in chapter thirteen, "No Room for Evil," further neopagan statements denying any clear distinction between good and evil.)

Whatever the source of the denial, neopagans make many moral judgments about history, personal life and public life. They are particularly strong in their condemnation of the "burnings," that is, the witchcraft trials and burning at the stake of so many in Europe and America. We can lament with them the injustice, but we might ask, "On what basis do you see these abuses as unjust or evil?"

Often neopagans are on the forefront of environmental issues and concerns. Since believers in Christ have not always cared for the preservation of the environment, neopagan and New Age voices are most heard on these matters. While we would maintain that preserving the environment is a real good, we might ask once again, "Is preserving the environment a real good and destroying the environment a real evil?" If so, how can neopagans and New Agers make this judgment without appealing to an absolute?

Through a friend, I met a couple in Berkeley, California, who were committed neopagans. He was a prominent leader in the largest neopagan group in the country at that time. We spent the whole evening talking, and the next day they sought me out again. We spent a productive afternoon talking over lunch and in a park there in Berkeley. Based on their own words and my observations, this couple clearly enjoyed the conversation. This instance and comments from others have illustrated the rarity of such wide-ranging, thoughtful, sustained dialogues between neopagans and informed believers in Christ. Too often believers are afraid to be in the vicinity of a witch and keep their distance.

I believe that New Agers and neopagans are often unaware of the profound tensions and contradictions in their positions and actually, at times, appreciate having them pointed out. I have often found honesty among the top New Age leaders and a willingness to admit profound problems. One such prominent leader, whom I regard as the most brilliant thinker of that persuasion, has said several times when I raised questions about fundamental issues, "I don't know. I'll have to think about that." He has also said that because of these and other questions he is considering coming back to the church.

Even though one might think it possible to live consistently with atheist, New Age or pagan relativist assumptions, I have not seen any such assumptions lived out in practice. In fact, I question whether it is possible for any of these theories to be consistently lived *or* thought. Despite the repudiation of moral absolutes in theory, each one of these groups brings universal judgments in by the back door. If they are unable to live what they advocate, does that not cast doubt on their theories? To the relativist one might say, as Peter Kreeft does:

> You talk about emancipating humanity from the terrible repressions of absolutism, and from all the effort you put into your missionary enterprise, one might have expected that you believed your message was really true, and teaching it was really good. But your message is that "there's nothing good or bad, but thinking makes it so." . . . You relativists preach against preaching. You're missionaries without a religion. . . . Either practice what you preach, or else preach what you practice. If you practice the relativism you preach, you'll stop preaching. If you preach what you practice, you'll start preaching . . . a real right and wrong.[22]

114

This inherent inconsistency provides a hole in the dike that may lead to a vast flood.

INTOLERANCE FOR THE INTOLERANT

One proponent of relativism was emphasizing the need for tolerance. When asked if there were limits to tolerance, this person eventually came to the conclusion (it seemed for the first time) that one can be "intolerant of the intolerant." The example of a justifiable object of intolerance was a fundamentalist Christian.

This "intolerance of the intolerant" reduces to the strange state of affairs that you should be tolerant of those with whom you agree and be intolerant of those with whom you disagree. The very people who need to be the object of tolerance—those with whom you disagree—are excluded from consideration. This unstable position may lead to the opposite of what its advocates profess to desire. It may actually lead to violence in the name of tolerance and relativism.

For instance, there is a movement in Berkeley, California, whose followers may have Mohawk haircuts or colored hair but who act as the enforcers not of conservative values but of liberal ones. They will beat up somebody caught smoking in a public place, wearing fur, eating meat or committing other breaches of the movement's guidelines on acceptable behavior.

Another radical environmental group commits acts of vandalism, including arson and the destruction of homes, offices, crops, logging equipment and sport-utility vehicles (SUVs). For instance, they vandalized a Burger King restaurant and two McDonald's restaurants. They set a fire at a ski resort, causing $12 million in damages and at an auto dealership destroying thirty SUVs.[23]

Perhaps these examples are aberrations and the problem will stop with them. However, I suspect that in the future there may be many reprisals, physical or otherwise, against those who disagree with the "absolutes" of relativism. Relativism is inherently unstable, and the tensions will force it either back to some absolute fixed values or, more likely, to forcing its "absolutes" on others.

CONSEQUENCES
OF THE DENIAL

BILL: *You've shown me how relativists are sometimes practically inconsistent, but what difference does a lack of absolutes make for my life? I don't believe in them and I'm doing fine.*

JOHN: *I believe there are only two options: God or meaninglessness.*

BILL: *I don't believe in God and I don't feel my life is meaningless.*

JOHN: *What I mean is that once you give up a fixed reference point outside this world, you have no basis to judge what is really meaningful.*

BILL: *But can't I just make up my own meaning for my life?*

JOHN: *Certainly, but that meaning has no binding force on anybody else. It's just what you feel is meaningful for you, but not the meaning of life.*

BILL: *You mean it is not the meaning to life but just my meaning?*

JOHN: *Yes, and even more, without God there is no basis for the dignity of people or morality.*

BILL: *Wow! That's a pretty sweeping statement. Why do you believe that?*

JOHN: *For the same reason I believe it's either God or meaninglessness. Let me show you why.*

෮~෴෨

The root problem of one's own age may seem abstract and difficult to grasp. I remember in a college chapel hearing Francis Schaeffer speak about this issue. My mind hurt. However, if you take the time to grasp the foundational point below, a window will open enabling you to see your present age more clearly. The most brilliant philosophers have come to the conclusion that if you give up belief in God, you are left with despair in the realms of meaning, dignity and morals.

MEANING

Atheist Jean-Paul Sartre (1905–1980) observed that no finite point has any meaning without an infinite reference point.[1] In figure 10.1 we see an infinite reference point and finite points representing people in their struggle to find meaning and morals for their lives.

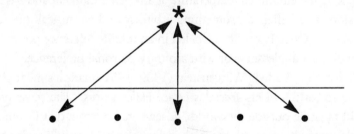

Figure 10.1. The struggle to find meaning and morals

Only if there is an infinite, eternal fixed point by which we can judge life can we talk about "the" meaning of life. Without this reference point, we can only judge things from our own individual, group or cultural perspective. If no finite point is meaningful without an infinite reference point, and if we accept that there is *no* infinite reference point, then life is truly meaningless. Sartre was willing to follow this option, declare life meaningless and sum up this view of life in the title of his book *Nausea*. Albert Camus (1913–1960), a fellow existentialist, followed Sartre's conclusion, and as a result he maintained that the only really serious question is whether or not to commit suicide. Mathematician and philosopher Bertrand Russell (1872–1970) held that atheists must build their lives on "unyielding despair."[2] Without this infinite reference point, there is no solid basis for meaning, dignity or morality, as we will soon see.

Many in our time, unwilling to embrace the cold despair of the existentialist, have chosen to believe the second option—that the meaning of life comes down to matters of purely personal preference. They would maintain that whatever is meaningful for me is meaningful just for me and whatever is meaningful for you is meaningful just for you. This view also disallows the argument that your meaning ought to be my meaning, because there is no ultimate rational basis by which you can justify this assertion. Consequently, there are as many meanings as there are people.

As appealing as this may at first sound to relativists, this makes for an uneven and distorted trip through life. Since the statement "meaningful for me" is based upon feeling or personal preference, I must go through life taking my emotional temperature at any given moment and base my decisions and beliefs on something arbitrary and whimsical: my emotional state. Once I give up the belief in an infinite reference point, I am left with meaninglessness or with arbitrary personal preference.

Philosopher Ludwig Wittgenstein (1889–1951) made a similar observation to Sartre's in his *Tractatus-Logico-Philosophicus:* "The sense of the world must lie outside the world." Elsewhere he wrote that if someone "could write a book on ethics which really was a book on ethics, this book would, with an explosion, destroy all the other books in the world."[3]

Notice that Wittgenstein underscored the importance of having a *revelation* from this infinite reference point—what he called "sense of the world" that comes from "outside the world." It would not help us, he pointed out, merely to know that there was an infinite reference point if we had no further knowledge about the meaning of life that only that infinite reference point could provide. We need a "book of ethics." Wittgenstein did not give serious consideration to the reality of such a revelation. He did, however, seem to realize the massive consequences if there were such a revelation.

The consequences of such a revelation are exactly what relativists seem determined to avoid. Jacques Derrida rejects what he calls "logo-centrism." This is not primarily a rejection of humanity's fixation on words, as you might expect, but a rejection of ultimate meaning or purpose. Related to this first denial he adds another: the denial of a "transcendental signified,"[4] or that which would provide a ground for absolute truth. Because Derrida denies this absolute reference point, he likewise denies ultimate meaning.

Once when my wife and I were traveling from Vienna to Budapest, we shared a train compartment with four young people. Two were Christian believers and two were atheists. Somehow the discussion moved to the topic of forgiveness and love. One young man, an atheist, asked the question, "Can't you be an atheist and love and forgive as much as anyone else?" He particularly wanted to get married and have a close and loving family life.

I responded, "Yes, you can be an atheist and love and forgive, but let's explore for a little bit what would make you desire to do so."

We talked about Sartre's infinite reference point, Wittgenstein's sense of the world that must come from outside the world, Camus's observation that the only really serious philosophical question was whether or not to commit suicide and atheist Russell's counsel to build your life on the basis of "unyielding despair." The young atheist soon came to see that there was no adequate basis in his atheism to either require love or to mandate forgiveness. There was no sufficient reason *why* he ought to live his life in the way he desired. Unless there is a sufficient reason why he should do these things, the cost at some point might be too great. He could choose to live without an adequate reason, but if times became difficult and relationships strained, what would necessitate love and forgiveness?

On the other hand, I encouraged him to consider Christ and the biblical view of life. Such a view is grounded in a triune God—Father, Son and Holy Spirit—existing in an eternal relationship of love. This places personality, as well as relationship and love, at the core of the cosmos. Christ came to demonstrate love by dying on the cross for our sins, and he called us to love, not only our neighbors and friends, but also our enemies. Christ encouraged us to pray, "Forgive us our debts, as we also have forgiven our debtors" (Mt 6:12). He said from the cross, "Father, forgive them; for they do not know what they are doing" (Lk 23:34). He also told us, "If you forgive others for their transgressions, your heavenly Father will also forgive you. But if you do not forgive others, then your Father will not forgive your transgressions" (Mt 6:14-15). We are called in the Great Commandment to love God and our neighbors (see Mt 22:37-39).

I asked the young atheist, "Which view of life is likely to encourage you most to be loving and forgiving?" He was listening intently, agreeing with what I said. At that moment we arrived at the border between Austria and Hungary and the border guards entered our car to check our passports. The young man was Canadian and for some reason needed a visa to go to Hungary, and so he had to be sent back to Vienna to get one. We arranged to meet him in Budapest the next day, but he was unable to come. I have often wondered what happened to him. But I could tell that this young atheist saw clearly the implications for his life if there were no fixed points by which he could orient himself in relationships or in the rest of life.

THE "TROUBLESOME" NEED FOR A FIXED POINT

This need for a fixed point is certainly not a modern or postmodern revelation. Blaise Pascal (1623–1662), in his *Pensées,* wrote about this need to have a fixed point from which we can judge moral issues:

> Those who lead disorderly lives tell those who are normal that [it] is they who deviate from nature, and think they are following nature themselves; just as those who are on board ship think that the people on shore are moving away. Language is the same everywhere: we need a fixed point to judge it. . . . When everyone is moving towards depravity, no one seems to be moving, but if someone stops, he shows up the others who are rushing on by acting as a fixed point.[5]

Once we give up an "infinite reference point," a "sense of the world" from "outside the world," a "transcendental signified" or a "fixed point," we are left with the dilemma of choosing between embracing meaninglessness or making up our own personal meanings.

LOSS OF HUMAN DIGNITY

Relativists often base their position on the concept that allowing each individual to live according to his or her own truth gives dignity to the individual. The opposite is true. Once you deny an infinite reference point by which to make ultimate judgments, it is far from clear on what basis you can ascribe dignity to any one person or to humanity as a whole. Statements about dignity become either meaningless or mere preference. Sartre described humankind as a "useless passion." Psychologist B. F. Skinner (1904–1990) wanted to go (as the title of his book suggests) *Beyond Freedom and Dignity,* reducing humans to nothing more than incarnated sets of conditioned responses. We can understand this further by comparing views on the origin and destiny of humankind through figure 10.2.

	Origin	Humankind	Destiny
Atheist	0	0	0
Secular Humanist	0	+	0
Theist	+	+	+

Figure 10.2. Three views of origin and destiny

For the consistent atheist, our origins spring out of the cosmic slime and our development staggers along by evolutionary lurches. Time, matter and chance somehow conspired to produce life and, through further chance mutations, produced humans. If that's true, then our origin is merely rocks and chemicals—intrinsically worth nothing. Our destiny is to return back to the same rocks and chemicals—thus, once again, worth nothing. What value or dignity does humankind possess in between origin and destiny? It would seem, based on the conclusions drawn by Sartre, Skinner and others, that the consistent answer is "Nothing."

While secular humanists (less consistent atheists) would agree that our origin is insignificant and our destiny is worthless, in between the two points, they would say, we can attribute great dignity to humankind (signified in the chart by the plus sign). But I believe that the reason humanists come to this conclusion is that they are made in the image of God and possess a moral law within, a conscience that recognizes that humans are endowed with significance. Absent an infinite reference point, however, the secular humanist lacks a basis other than sentiment on which to claim dignity for humans.

In contrast, the believer in Christ and in the Bible *has* a solid basis for the dignity of all humans. We are created by a God who is worthy of worship. Our origin is a giant plus. We are created in the image of that same God. Therefore, we have an intrinsic worth and dignity based not on what we do but on who we are. This worth and dignity cannot be taken away from us because it is intrinsic. We have value because of our Creator. Furthermore, the use of our lives matters because we are of such great worth, and our destiny is eternal, either for salvation or judgment. Because our origin is worthy, we have worth and our destiny matters.

As humans, we are important, not only because we have dignity, but also because of our destiny. Our dignity is related to our origin as well as our destiny. This explains why our culture—established on biblical values—places high value on human rights. In other cultures the communal is everything and the individual is nothing. In one Eastern culture, for example, human life is "as light as a feather."

We can also see the contrasting worldviews more clearly by studying their views of life and death.

	Origin	Humankind	Destiny
Atheist	Death	Life	Death
Believer	Life	Life	Life

Figure 10.3. Two views of life and death

According to the atheist, life comes from nonlife through evolution.

Our origin, in other words, is out of death. And since there is no life after death, our destiny is death. What then, in this view, is the point or value of life? Life is merely an unnecessary, temporary interruption in the midst of cosmic death. For the believer, on the other hand, our origin is out of life—the living God is our Creator. Our destiny in Christ is eternal life. Death is a temporary interruption in the midst of cosmic life.

Notice the radical contrasts between these views of life. Once you give up belief in an absolute—an infinite reference point or meaning from outside the world—there are profound consequences for both our human dignity and the meaning of life.

LOSS OF MORALS

The loss of absolutes in morality comes from this same root problem. Once you give up an infinite reference point, morality becomes either meaningless or can be created out of essentially arbitrary personal preferences. Because values are mere preferences, the values one chooses cannot be imposed on others without provoking the inevitable question "Who are you to impose your values on me?" or "Says who?" Novelist Feodor Dostoyevsky (1821–1881), in *The Brothers Karamazov,* offered the startling insight: "If there is no God, everything is permitted."

Allan Bloom, in his book *The Closing of the American Mind,* pointed to a paradox in the relativist view of things. On the one hand, universities throughout the world encourage an endless openness to whatever strange and bizarre views people may hold. Students are encouraged to be ever learning but are never encouraged to actually learn anything objectively true. Strangely, this endless openness leads to a kind of closing, a closing of the mind to the concept of ever arriving at "true truth."

G. K. Chesterton characteristically put this pursuit of open-mindedness in perspective. He always thought the purpose of "opening the mind as of opening the mouth is to shut it again on something solid."[6]

Steve Turner, a believer in Christ, has written a poem that describes the relativistic climate in which we live.

Creed
We believe in Marxfreudanddarwin.
We believe everything is O.K.
As long as you don't hurt anyone
To the best of your definition of hurt
And to the best of your knowledge. . . .

We believe that all religions are basically the same
At least the one that we read was.
They all believe in love and goodness.
They only differ on matters of
Creation, sin, heaven, hell, God and salvation. . . .

We believe that each man must find the truth
That is right for him.
Reality will adapt accordingly
The universe will readjust.
History will alter.
We believe that there is no absolute truth
Excepting the truth that there is no absolute truth.

We believe in the rejection of creeds.[7]

Turner's poem is certainly humorous, but it is also insightful. Note particularly the thoughts in the last stanza, accurately reflecting the contemporary belief that we create our own reality.

CONFORMING DESIRE TO TRUTH OR TRUTH TO DESIRE

C. S. Lewis, in *The Abolition of Man,* described the two roads that people follow:

There is something which unites magic and applied science while separating both from the "wisdom" of earlier ages. For wise men of old, the cardinal problem had been how to *conform the soul to reality,* and the solution had been knowledge, self-discipline, and virtue. For magic and applied science alike, the problem is how to *subdue reality to the wishes of men:* the solution is technique.[8]

In short, we must choose whether we believe that reality is what we make it to be or whether there is an ultimate reality to which we must respond. The two roads set before us are: (1) conform the soul to reality, or (2) subdue reality to our wishes. On the first road we find God's grace at work, conforming our desires to the truth. On the second road we find magic, applied science, the human potential movement, Eastern religion, neopaganism and postmodernism at work, all attempting to conform truth to the individual's desires. On the first road truth is solid and knowable; truth is that which corresponds to reality. We need to know our place in that reality and conform ourselves to the God who created it. On the second road our desires are sovereign, and we can rationalize our behavior or redefine reality in order to do what we want.

If we take the second road, it can lead inexorably to the position described by novelist and critic Aldous Huxley (1894–1963):

> I had motives for not having the world to have meaning. And consequently, I assumed it had none and was able to find satisfying reasons for this assumption. The philosopher who finds no meaning in the world isn't concerned exclusively with a problem in pure metaphysics. He's also concerned to prove there's no valid reason why he personally should not do as he wants to do. For myself and as no doubt for my contemporaries, the philosophy of meaninglessness was essentially an instrument of liberation—the liberation we desired was from a certain system of morality. . . . We objected to the morality because it interfered with our sexual freedom. The supporters of this system claimed that in some way it embodied a Christian meaning of the world. There was one admirably simple method of refuting these people and at the same time justifying ourselves in our erotic revolt. We would deny the world had any meaning whatever.[9]

The Nature of This Debate

This debate between two worldviews is not merely a theoretical war of words; it has profound practical consequences. As Huxley openly admitted, people may take positions not only for intellectual reasons but also for reasons of justifying their own desires.

Relativism, as we are already seeing, poses practical problems. Once you give up a fixed, transcendent reference point, there is nothing to stop you from creating your own meaning and nothing to cause you to value people—unless, of course, you choose to do so solely as an act of the will. There is also nothing to prevent you from creating your own morality or having no morality at all, nothing to stop the plummet into meaninglessness or into viewing people as a "useless passion" (Sartre).

Many severe difficulties result from denying absolutes, among them the problem indicated in the last stanza of Turner's poem:

> We believe that there is no absolute truth
> Excepting the truth that there is no absolute truth.

This self-contradictory quality of relativism—and the chaos that ensues—is the subject of the next chapter.

RELATIVISM SELF-DESTRUCTS

BILL: *I see that there are real consequences to living without God. Can't we just face them and move on?*

JOHN: *Not so fast. Consequences are more than practical; there are profound logical problems with relativism. In many areas it is self-refuting. It saws off the branch on which it is sitting.*

౦ᄍᄍᄼ

The Greek philosopher Gorgias (c. 483–376 B.C.) claimed that all statements are false. Immediately there is a problem with this statement: if it is true that "all statements are false," then that statement itself is false. This same kind of absurd contradiction lies at the foundation of relativism.

SELF-REFUTING

Relativism is at its root self-contradictory. Its claims are self-refuting. It is absurd, after all, to say or believe that the premise "There are no absolutes" makes an absolute statement about all of reality. The logical status of the statement is that of a *universal negative*. Making a comprehensive, absolute, universal negation is equivalent to maintaining that there are "absolutely no absolutes." It has the same absurd quality as the statement "I hold to the truth that there are no truths" or the claim "It is wrong to hold that there is anything wrong."[1]

Relativists consistently stand guilty of the philosophical sin of making exceptions to their own absolute rules. When confronted with the self-contradictory nature of their statements, advocates of relativism often make light of the point. In my experience it is passed off with a joke or by dodging the issue.

In seminary I had a professor, Dr. John Gerstner, who taught a course on the cults. The class met for three hours once a week. During those three hours, Dr. Gerstner role-played a cult member for the whole class. He would not easily yield, even when we had a good argument. Once we spent the whole class period debating an issue with him. Along the way we raised an answer to his question and he responded with a vague "No, no, no—that will never do." So we went on to another approach. At the end of the three hours, we asked him to give us the answer. It was the very thing we had raised earlier. We protested, "But that is just what we said earlier and you said, 'No, no, no—that will never do.'" Dr. Gerstner responded to us, "Did you expect me to give up so easily? You had a good point, but you gave up when you needed to drive it home."

So it is with the relativists we encounter. After they attempt an evasive maneuver such as described above, we may want to be gently persistent. Perhaps we could point out that there have been many times in the history of philosophy when the fundamental assumption of a position was shown to be contradictory and that position had to be given up for lost or severely modified. For instance, the philosophy of logical positivism at one point relied on the "verifiability principle." This principle stated, "Only those statements are meaningful that are true by definition or empirically verifiable." The statement that a "bachelor is an unmarried man" is true by definition. Logical positivists used this verifiability principle as a hammer to question the meaningfulness of ethical and theological statements. Ethical statements, they asserted, were not true by definition, nor were they empirically verifiable, and therefore they were meaningless. This position worked until someone pointed out that the verifiability principle was itself neither true by definition nor empirically verifiable; therefore, on its own terms it was meaningless. Thus it had to be renounced or brought back in a much softer, less dogmatic form.

CONTEXTUALISM

The self-refuting character of philosophical positions is not always so obvious. Often it is concealed in a barrage of words and assertions, some of which are partially true. A valuable principle to remember, however, is that a partial truth taken as the whole truth becomes an untruth. This is particularly true with the school of philosophical thought known as *contextualism*.

One of the central assertions of postmodernism is that all philosophical, religious or ethical claims are embedded in a cultural context. So far, so good. We are inevitably affected by the cultural context in which we live—our language, history and cultural ways and practices.

Radical contextualists go far beyond this valid point. They insist that we are so embedded in our cultural contexts that we cannot escape them, that our culture determines our beliefs. Since different cultures and religious perspectives disagree on what is true, the contextualists conclude that it is impossible to settle our differences.

Certainly, people do disagree over what is true, good and beautiful. This is a readily apparent observation. Is it, though, impossible to find any way to settle our differences? This assertion—that it is impossible to settle our differences, whether asserted directly or implied—has become an absolute statement on which the contextualist rests his or her claims. And what follows is often another absolute assertion: All our knowledge is relative to our culture.

William Dembski pointed out the fallacy in radical contextualism:

Hardcore contextualism asserts that context alone determines what is true, good, and right. In so doing, hardcore contextualism makes a universal claim, which, therefore, can be applied to it. Yet, when applied to it, hardcore contextualism strips itself of any claims to universality. If context alone determines what is true, then there can be no universal truths that hold across contexts. Yet, by speaking for all contexts at once, hardcore contextualism claims itself to be a universal truth that there are no universal truths. This is the fallacy of contextualism.[2]

True, there is a certain advantage in hard-core contextualism: no one outside your context can challenge you philosophically, religiously or ethically. Subscribing to this school of thought allows you to do whatever you want. You can also have all the fire of a prophet putting forth moral judgments based on your personal or "community" standards while at the same time making yourself immune from criticism by any other culture, community or religion.

⌘

BILL: *Aren't you aware that all our knowledge is relative to our culture?*

JOHN: *Is the claim that "all our knowledge is relative to culture" absolute or relative?*

BILL: *I can see what you are getting at, and I am not going to fall into your trap. I am just saying that our culture shapes our thinking and many cultures have opposing views. Who are we to say that we are right?*

JOHN: *You are backing off from your original position because you know what I would say: If all knowledge is relative to culture, then there is at least one piece of knowledge that is not relative—that statement. On the other hand, if only some knowledge is relative to culture, then what part is and what part isn't?*

BILL: *Come on. You know we are all shaped by our culture.*

JOHN: *I agree; we are shaped by our culture. However, your very awareness of this problem suggests that you might be able to escape your culture's influence over your views. Can't you critique your culture?*

BILL: *Of course I can.*

JOHN: *Then your culture's influence is not absolute, only relative.*

BILL: *Explain what you mean.*

JOHN: *If you can stand above your culture to critique it, then your culture's influence is not total. That's all I'm trying to say at this point—that your very statement "all knowledge is relative to culture" assumes that there is some knowledge not relative to culture. That statement also hints that somehow you can get out of your cultural entrapment long enough to make that statement— and perhaps a whole lot of other ones as well.*

OBJECTIVELY NO OBJECTIVITY

On the basis of self-contradictory "truths," many in our culture have come to confidently hold the belief that it is impossible to know objective truth. However, while it is true that we are all subjects and therefore unable to escape the subject-object dilemma, does this mean that we cannot really and truly know any object? Is objective truth forever banished from consideration?

There is much to be said about the difficulties of objectivity and much we can learn from reading postmodernists on this subject. Let us keep in mind, however, that the statement "There is no objective truth" claims to be an objective statement of truth (when it is not offered as a statement of merely private opinion). It is tantamount to saying, "I can objectively say that there is no objectivity." It is also important to note that the arguments and evidences that demonstrate the difficulties of total objectivity require the assumption that we can have a significant overlap of understanding with the author so that we can understand the contentions being asserted.

The question may be asked, is it possible—given that we are finite, contextually influenced, prejudiced and biased—to arrive at an approximation of objective truth? Granted, we cannot claim to have absolute objectivity; the only one who has absolute objectivity is God. We can define truth as *that which corresponds to reality as perceived by God.* Perhaps it is the last phrase "as perceived by God," coupled with the fact that we are not God, that lies behind the current debates. Donald Carson, in *The Gagging of God,* said, "We may not aspire to absolute knowledge of the sort only Omniscience may possess, but the 'approximation' may be so good that it is adequate for placing human beings on the moon. . . . The point of all such models is that although none of us ever knows any complicated thing exhaustively, we can know some things truly."[3]

Carson illustrated his point by saying that a child can understand "God loves the world" (Jn 3:16) truly (though partially) and can grow in a more complete (though never comprehensive) knowledge of God's love throughout all of life. There can be, to use a phrase of Hans-Georg Gadamer (1900–2002), an increasing "fusion of horizons" between the text and his or her understanding the reality of it.

As Carson alluded in the quote above, science and technology strive for objectivity and achieve it to a remarkable degree, enough (for instance) to put a man on the moon. Science attempts to face the problem of objectivity squarely. It requires the replication of results, repeatability, and blind and double-blind experiments. All these methodological demands force approaches that can overcome bias, prejudice and the experimenters' imposition of their theories on reality. In many ways science acknowledges the postmodern problem. Yet is there anyone who would want to say that the "objective truth" that "smoking causes cancer" is up for grabs?[4]

During the discussion that follows, keep in mind that the statement "There is no objective truth" is self-refuting. Remembering this point is necessary because the tangle of problems with relativism only gets worse.

YOU CANNOT COMMUNICATE THAT
YOU CANNOT COMMUNICATE

Some in postmodernism, as well as those in the New Age and neopagan movements, stress the ambiguity of language. The more extreme view—structuralism—asserts that words refer only to other words (which refer to other words . . . and so on). This means that there is no inherent meaning to a text and furthermore that there is no meaning that is superior to another meaning. Jacques Derrida and Paul de Man often emphasize that a text can support mutually incompatible interpretations. Richard Rorty (b. 1931) contended, "It is all words, all the way down."[5]

To be sure, this is a complex topic, but the first thing that must be noted is that even the most extreme writers, such as Derrida and Rorty, assume that their words are saying something definite and are offended when someone misinterprets their words. Derrida, for instance, wrote a ninety-three-page response to an eight-page critique of his views, offended that he had been misunderstood. Barbara Johnson said in the translator's introduction to Derrida's *Dissemination,* "Derrida thus finds himself in the uncomfortable position of attempting to account for an error by means of tools derived from that very error. For it is not possible to show that the belief in truth is an error without implicitly believing in the notion of Truth."[6] Derrida, at one point in *Writing and Difference,* admitted that it is impossible to reject a logocentric approach without having to assume that approach.[7]

Any denial of the meaningfulness of words uses words to make that denial. It assumes that you can communicate that you cannot communicate. I have often found that intelligent people have not thought through the implications of what they are saying. Once I had a long discussion with the leader of a New Age think tank who was maintaining that language was hopelessly obscure and equivocal. It is hard to distill the conversation in a short space, but it went something like this (A=Art; N=New Age thinker):

A: You say that language is hopelessly obscure and equivocal. I certainly understand the difficulties. I have often said that there are always three messages in any communication: (1) what I intend to say, (2) what I actually say and (3) what you hear.

N: I am not just talking about a failure of communication on your part. I am talking about an intrinsic problem with language.

A: Okay, there is a real possibility that the meaning of some of the words I am using differ from the meaning you give to the same words. Couldn't we work to define the words so we have the same or almost the same meaning?

N: No. Because of my cultural context, background and experience, I can never have the same meaning as you.

A: Okay, perhaps never 100 percent the same, but do you think that we could get to 90 percent or 80 percent? Do you think we have 0 percent overlap in meaning?

N: I suppose not.

A: In fact, what percent of what we are talking about right this second, in the words I am saying now, do you misunderstand?

N: Good point. Let's talk about some other issues.

Keep in mind that despite the difficulties of speaking across "horizons"— across cultures, mindsets and languages—we can, if we try, have real communication. To deny that we can communicate is to communicate that we cannot communicate. It is using words to deny that we can understand words, which again is self-refuting.

When you find yourself in a situation like this, you might ask your conversation partner, "Does it matter to you that you are unable to affirm your fundamental assumption without denying it?" Or you might ask, "Is relativism true and a belief in absolutes false? If so, there is *something* objectively and absolutely true, isn't there?" With a little thought and creativity, you can come up with a follow-up question that gently and lovingly presses your point home.

REJECTING RATHER THAN REFUTING

One of the favorite defenses of relativists is to *reject* the person who believes in absolutes rather than *refute* what is being said. They attempt to reduce you and your argument by the use of labeling: "You're just an absolutist." They may even resort to name-calling: "You're a narrow-minded bigot."

C. S. Lewis dubbed this defensive tactic "Bulverism" in his essay by that name in *First and Second Things*. The name of the essay comes from an imaginary character, Ezekiel Bulver, "whose destiny was determined at age five when he heard his mother say to his father—who had been maintaining that two sides of a triangle were together greater than that of the third—'Oh you say that because you are a man.' " At that moment, Ezekiel Bulver assures us,

> "There flashed across my opening mind that *refutation is no neces-sary part of an argument.* Assume that your opponent is wrong, and then explain his error and the world will be at your feet. Attempt to prove that he is wrong or (worse still) try to find out if he is wrong or right, and the national dynamism of our age will thrust you to the wall." That is how Bulver became one of the makers of the Twentieth Century.[8]

"Bulverism" is a convenient and often-used ploy. It is much easier, and safer, to reject and call someone names than to try to refute that person's views. You can see it everywhere in the academic world, on television, in movies, in newspapers and in politics.[9] In fact, Lewis said that he saw Bulverism at work in "every political argument" and that "until Bulver-ism is crushed, reason can have no effective part in human affairs."[10] So the next time someone attacks your religious belief with name-calling— "narrow-minded," "intolerant," "you need a crutch," "naive" and so on— you can say, "That is mere Bulverism." Or you can say, "You know, it is much easier to call me names than to show that I am wrong." Or say, "Perhaps your case is so weak that all you can do is throw dust in the air."

Dorothy Sayers was profoundly aware of how people reject rather than refute. In "Selections from the Pantheon Papers," she wrote a satir-ical piece about some newly discovered papers that described a strange society devoted to unbelief (similar to *The Screwtape Letters* by Lewis). Some of the cynical advice given in these papers include the following:

> Remember when cultivating your cold bed of Polemic, never de-fine, never expound, never discuss, only assert and assume. Where there is dogma there is always a *possible basis* for agreement; where there is explanation there is argument, there may be victory and

the dreadful prospect of peace. Again, it is often unwise, and always unnecessary, to invite examination into the merits of your case. . . . Strive earnestly to confuse every issue. . . . Any effort to oppose a new idea on the specious pretext that it is nasty, false, dangerous, or wrong should be promptly stigmatized as heresy-hunting, medieval obscurantism, or suburban prejudice.[11]

Bulverism is, however, a truly democratic game; it can be played both ways. You can argue (using evidence) that the opposite is the case. The next time a relativist calls your belief "a crutch," you might try responding with one of the following:

- "You know, relativism is just wish fulfillment."
- "Relativism is an opiate of the conscience."
- "Relativism is just a giant Oedipus complex, wishing for the death of the heavenly Father."

When my wife, Connie, and I were on our honeymoon, we stayed in delightful grass huts at the Hotel Oa Oa in Bora Bora. The manager, when he heard that we were in ministry, stated flatly, "I think religion is a crutch." I responded quietly but firmly, "I think atheism is a crutch," and went on to explain it as I have just described. My response effectively neutralized this often-used, discussion-stopping criticism, and we were then able to have a productive interchange.

CHRONOLOGICAL SNOBBERY

Relativists also sometimes charge, "Your view is old-fashioned." This implies that, because a certain belief was held in a previous age, it is false. If you encounter such a charge, you could respond by asking, "Just because something is old or held in an earlier age, does that make it necessarily false?" Or ask, "Does the fact that a view is new make it necessarily true?" This kind of response may provoke a good discussion.

One of the obstacles that C. S. Lewis had to overcome in order to come to faith was his own chronological snobbery. What could a two-thousand-year-old religion have to do with him in the middle of the twentieth century? Chronological snobbery was defined by Lewis as "the uncritical acceptance of the intellectual climate of our own age and the assumption that whatever has gone out-of-date is on that count discredited."[12] Through the arguments of philosopher Owen Barfield (1898–1997), Lewis eventually came to understand the need to ask questions like these:

- Why did this idea go out of date?
- Was it ever refuted?
- If so, by whom, where and how conclusively?

He came to the further understanding that our age is a mere period and that it has its own particular illusions.

As an antidote to chronological snobbery, Lewis advocated letting the "breezes of the centuries" blow through our minds:

> It is a good rule after reading a new book never to allow yourself another new one till you have read an old one in between. If that is too much for you, you should at least read one old one to every three new ones.
>
> Every age has its own outlook. It is especially good at seeing certain truths and especially liable to make certain mistakes. We all, therefore, need the books that will correct the characteristic mistakes of our own period. . . .
>
> None of us can fully escape this blindness, but we shall certainly increase it, and weaken our guard against it, if we read only modern books. . . .
>
> The only palliative is to keep the clean sea breeze of the centuries blowing through our minds and this can be done only by reading old books.[13]

You might try exploring this idea of cultural blind spots with relativists. Some have said the postmodernism is a "mere mood" that may soon pass away. Perhaps you can help postmodernists see that their view, at least in part, may be just another fad in the long history of ideas.

BILL: *Do you want us to turn back the clock to that archaic, outmoded belief in absolute truth?*

JOHN: *If a clock is not telling the right time, you need to turn it back. But apart from that, do you assume that just because my view has been held in ancient times it is false?*

BILL: *What could a two-thousand-year-old faith have to say to us today?*

JOHN: *Well, a great deal, I think. Would you say that a religious view is false just because it is old? Certainly there are many past views that have been shown to be false. Do you think that faith in Christ has been demonstrated as false? If so, where and how conclusively?*

BILL: *Well, I just don't want to be bound by the past. I want to be free to explore new ideas.*

JOHN: *Are you aware that those who neglect past ideas tend to be enslaved to the recent past? Often the views of this generation tend to be shaped by the previous generation of teachers, and they tend to be shaped by the generation previous to them and so on. Perhaps your views are not as new or free as you think they are.*

BILL: *Anyone blind to the new postmodern wave must be irrelevant.*

JOHN: *It seems that all you can do is call my views outmoded. Don't you realize that your own views will soon be the same?*

The ironic problem with relativism and postmodernism is that, if they succeed, then they fail. C. S. Lewis said that it is no use to "try to prove that all proofs are invalid. If you fail, you fail. If you succeed, then you fail even more—for the proof that all proofs are invalid must be invalid itself." Relativists are in the absurd situation of sawing off the branch on which they are sitting.[14]

UNPROVABLE

Relativism has another devastating difficulty: it is unprovable. The statement "There are no absolutes" is a universal negative statement, and such statements are often harder to prove than positive ones.

Take, for instance, the statement "There is no gold in Alaska." How could you prove the statement true? You would first have to determine the precise borders of Alaska and how deep Alaska goes, then dig up and examine every cubic inch of Alaska. If there was one cubic inch of Alaska that remained unexamined, then you could not make your negative claim.

On the other hand, take the positive assertion "There is gold in Alaska." To prove the statement, you need to find only one piece of gold. If there were any gold in Alaska, you would presumably find it sooner than if you were proving there was none.

Similarly, what would you have to know in order to say "There are no absolutes" or "There is no God"? In a word, you would need to know *everything*. If there was one thing you did not know, that one thing might be an absolute. We are obviously so far from knowing everything there is to be known that the relativists' assertion is unprovable. The best a relativist could say is "I do not think there are any absolutes." To which we could respond, "Since you are not certain that everything is relative, let me show you why I think there are absolutes."

Remember, it is possible that the term "absolutes" might get in the way of a discussion, since "absolutes" might imply absolutism in the relativist's mind. It may be more helpful to use other terms, such as "infinite reference point," "sense to the world from outside the world," "objective truth and morality" or just "fixed points by which we can orient ourselves."

ARROGANT

The dogmatic claims "There are no absolutes" and "There is no God" are not only contradictory and unprovable; they are also arrogant. As we saw above, this universal negative statement implies the possession of infinite knowledge.

One time my friend Jerry Root asked the famous atheist Madalyn Murray O'Hair a question: "How much of that which there is to be known do you claim to know—maybe 10 percent?"

O'Hair laughed and said, "Okay, 10 percent."

He then asked, "Is it possible that God might exist and be part of that 90 percent of reality that you admittedly do not know?"

O'Hair paused and was silent for about a minute. Then she said, "A qualified 'no' "—and quickly moved on to another question.

Observing the difficulty of proving the universal negative does not, of course, prove that there is a God, but it might open up closed people to reconsidering their assumptions. One young atheist law student received a letter containing the "gold in Alaska" analogy given above and wrote back saying he had attended church that week. He said that perhaps he had rejected belief in God without seriously considering it.

Of course, the atheist could come back with an argument that because of the problem of evil or inconsistencies in our view of God, our view is impossible to rationally defend or is contradictory. I am convinced that all such attempts have failed.[15]

While we admittedly know little of what there is to be known, that little knowledge is enough to discover "gold in Alaska"—or the pearl of great price, the hidden treasure of Christ. In other words, we do not need to know everything in order to discover something. As believers we profess that we have come to a knowledge of God through Christ and that we have been privileged to receive his revelation in Scripture. The dogmatic relativist, on the other hand, makes an implicit claim to know everything. That is arrogant.

Perhaps the relativist you are talking to has not yet realized the implications of what he or she is saying, so you need to approach these questions in a loving manner.

EVERYBODY'S RIGHT
AND NOBODY'S RIGHT

BILL: *So what? Who needs logic? Didn't Emerson say that consistency is the hobgoblin of small minds?*

JOHN: *I think "foolish consistency" was the hobgoblin. But anyway, the problem is that people are selective in the areas where they want to throw out reason. It's easy to say "Who needs logic?" in a college classroom, but it's impossible to live, act, talk or think without reason.*

⚭

My older son has always loved seafood; my younger son dislikes it. My older son loves mushrooms; my younger son does not. These are purely matters of taste and not big issues. Nobody goes to war to prove seafood tastes better than some other kind of food. When it comes to matters of taste, whatever is true for you is true for you, and whatever is true for me is true for me. In this realm of taste, everybody can be "right."

The serious problem with relativism, however, is that it reduces universal matters of *truth* to the same level as matters of taste and preference. Unlike the choices on a restaurant menu, real-world ideas and ideologies have consequences, for ideas and ideologies form attitudes, and those attitudes form behaviors. How I think about you and how I treat you can start, on a greater or smaller scale, a war. In the real world, what we believe *does* matter.

Relativists insist that all ideas and beliefs and ethics fall into the category of personal taste. But on what grounds do they make this assertion?

More importantly, can it possibly be that my preferred beliefs are true and that your preferred beliefs, though diametrically opposite my beliefs, are also true?

MATTERS TOO IMPORTANT TO DISMISS

Many issues in religion and ethics are mutually contradictory, and one or the other option must be true independent of anyone's preference. This is the point at which relativism collapses in contradictions. While insisting, "Everyone is right," at the same time it asserts that nobody is really right. To the relativist, no one can claim what Francis Schaeffer called "true truth"—truth that is true whether you believe it or not.

But again, when it comes to the most fundamental issues of religion and ethics, one option or another must be true apart from my preference or yours. For both views, if mutually contradictory, cannot be true at the same time.

Consider the issue of God's existence. If the God of the Bible exists, then no amount of insistence that he does not exist is going to make him cease to exist. Equally, if the God of the Bible does *not* exist, no amount of insistence that he exists will make him exist.

The same is true of the immortal soul. Either there is some kind of personal existence after death or there is not. If there is continued personal existence after death, no amount of unbelief will alter the fact. If there is no personal existence after death, no amount of belief will cause it to happen.

EITHER/OR OR BOTH-AND

It is urgent that we explore our options when it comes to the matter of the nature of reality—whether it has an absolute or a relative quality—and also that we recognize the full consequences of each option. Relativism seems to imply that contradictory religious or philosophical views can both be true.

In fact, there are only three options when it comes to the nature of reality:

1. Reality is noncontradictory.
2. Reality is contradictory.
3. Reality is noncontradictory in some areas but contradictory in other areas.[1]

REALITY IS NONCONTRADICTORY

The first option is that reality is noncontradictory. The law of noncontradiction is this: A cannot be non-A at the same time and in the same relationship. For instance, a person cannot be in Washington, D.C., and not be in Washington, D.C., at the same time. On the other hand, you *can* be both a father and a son (that is, a son to your father) in different relationships. But you cannot be a father and not be a father in relation to your own son.

Classical Christian tradition has held that the law of noncontradiction applies both to God and to creation. Some assert that the law of noncontradiction does not apply to God and therefore contradictory statements can be affirmed of him at the same time and in the same relationship. If this is the case, then God is holy and God is not holy in the same sense. Or you could say that God is good and God is not good. Or that God exists and God does not exist. Everything that can be affirmed about God can also be negated in the same sense.

Similarly, if creation is by nature contradictory, then we cannot have any knowledge about created reality at all. Anything we could affirm we could negate, in the same sense. "The tree is there" and "The tree is not there" would both be true.

Once again we see that the relativist relies on arguments that are self-refuting because any attempt to deny the law of noncontradiction requires this very law in order to make its denials. Otherwise the statement "the law of noncontradiction does not apply to reality" could in fact be used as an affirmation of its truth.

As Christians, however, we must affirm that the law of noncontradiction operates in all reality, including statements about God. To say "God exists," as we do, is not the same as saying, "God does not exist." This affirmation of the law of noncontradiction is not an importation of Greek philosophy. That I believe the noncontradiction law does not mean that I have become an "Aristotelian" or that I endorse "modernism." We can defend rationality while rejecting rationalism. The law of noncontradiction is as much rooted in Hebrew thought as in Greek thought. Antithesis— the concept that mutually exclusive things cannot both be true—is a central theme of both the Old and New Testaments.

In the beginning of Genesis, for instance, the basic temptation was a negation of what God had affirmed. God said of the forbidden tree, "In the day that you eat from it you will surely die" (Gen 2:17). The serpent maintained, "You surely will not die!" (3:4). Which should we believe? Can both be true in the same sense? Certainly not; this shows the antithesis between the truth and a lie.

Consider the Ten Commandments. Does "You shall have no other gods before Me" mean we are commanded to worship other gods? Does "You shall not commit adultery" mean adultery is permissible or "You shall not steal" mean stealing is actually all right? Each one of these commands depends on the law of noncontradiction, or antithesis.

One of Francis Schaeffer's emphases was the importance of antithesis. The biblical view, he contended, involves acknowledging a contradiction between the true and false prophet, between right and wrong, between good and evil, between salvation and judgment, between the broad way and the narrow way. J. I. Packer commented, "For Schaeffer the most tragic—because the most anti-human—thing in life was the willful refusal by a human being to face the antithesis or rather the series of antitheses with which God in Holy Scripture confronts us, and in this perception I think he was right."[2]

Not only does a denial of the law of noncontradiction actually affirm it; in fact, any such denial must be seen for what it is: forced and temporary. For example, a professor might deny logic in a classroom lecture, then proceed to open the door to leave the lecture hall, assuming that the door is there as opposed to not being there at the same time. The same professor drives home and looks both ways before pulling onto the highway, assuming that the large truck coming at sixty miles per hour is there as opposed to not being there. The professor assumes that the university contract promising a salary of $70,000 is not the same as one promising $35,000. Yes, any denial of the law of noncontradiction, antithesis or logic is theoretical and temporary. C. S. Lewis said, "Unless all that we take to be knowledge is illusion, we must hold that in thinking we are not reading rationality into an irrational universe, but responding to a rationality with which the universe has always been saturated."[3]

Let me emphasize again that the law of noncontradiction is not merely Western, Aristotelian or modernist. It is universal. Even where there is not much emphasis on philosophical kinds of questions, or a self-conscious awareness of the nature of knowledge, logic is still implicit and may become explicit. For example, though Chinese philosophy did not generally pursue knowledge for its own sake, particularly because it did not make a clear distinction between the individual and the universe, some participating in it did value logic and clear moral standards. For example, the Chinese Later Mohist School held to a commonsense worldview, discussed the nature of our knowledge, and argued against moral, philosophical and linguistic relativism.[4]

Mozi, "Master Mo" (480–390 B.C.), founded this Mohist school, pursuing various subjects. Note what he said about morality:

> When one advances claims, one must first establish a standard of assessment. To make claims in the absence of such a standard is like trying to establish on the surface of a spinning potter's wheel where the sun will rise and set. *Without a fixed standard, one cannot clearly ascertain what is right and wrong* or what is beneficial or harmful.[5]

Mozi not only argued against moral relativism but also believed that the material world was knowable and that objective morality was the direct source of knowledge. He and his followers were critical of the Chinese sophists, the School of Names. Mohists argued that propositions must tally with facts and used the law of noncontradiction to show that these sophists were playing with words, trying to eliminate the distinction between right and wrong.

The Mohists made great contributions to the development of logic in ancient China.[6] This is just one example demonstrating that logic and the law of noncontradiction are not simply products of the West but also had their defenders in the East. "Western logic" and "Eastern logic" are not so mutually exclusive as has been maintained.

The skepticism about objective truth and whether it can be known is not new. The Sophist Protagoras (485–410 B.C.) maintained (according to Plato) that "man is the measure of all things" and that anything "is to me as it appears to me and is to you such as it appears to you." He and other Sophists held that truth was subjective and values likewise a matter of taste. Gorgias, on the other hand, was a complete skeptic. He held that nothing exists and that, if anything did exist, it would be incomprehensible, and that, even if it were comprehensible, it could not be communicated. Words were not a means of grasping reality but a tool for persuading and manipulating others.

Far from the present postmodern skepticism about objective truth and morality being something new and bold, it is a return to an ancient way of thinking. Hannah Arendt contrasted the ancient and modern relativists: "The most striking difference between ancient and modern sophists is that the ancients were satisfied with a passing victory of argument at the expense of truth, whereas the moderns want a more lasting victory at the expense of reality."[7]

❧

BILL: *Don't you know that the whole postmodern wave rejects logic and shows how arguments are just used to manipulate people?*

JOHN: *I don't think you can affirm your position or deny mine without using logic. You have to use logic to deny logic, use reason to deny reason and use the* law of noncontradiction to deny the law of noncontradiction.

BILL: *But you can't prove the law of noncontradiction, can you?*

JOHN: *I suppose I can't prove it. Some issues are so basic that they are axioms—you can't prove anything else without them. If you give up logic or reason, then you give up all knowledge and ought to give up thinking or talking because all these assume the law of noncontradiction.*

BILL: *But I reject reason—that's modernist.*

JOHN: *You can use your reason to deny reason. You can deny logic theoretically, but I don't think you can or will deny it practically. Are you going to step out in front of that large truck speeding down the road, saying that truck is there and not there? Do you think that chair you are sitting on is there or not there or both?*

REALITY IS CONTRADICTORY

The second option in regard to the nature of reality is that reality is contradictory at the core. This view is often held in some forms of Hinduism and Buddhism and is echoed in New Age thinking. The view that the nature of reality is contradictory is rooted in the belief that all is one—sometimes expressed as the principle of nondistinction. In this view there is no need for the law of noncontradiction, because everything is in some sense identical.

For the Zen Buddhist, all conceptualization, whether words or raw concepts, fails to touch reality. It is only by short-circuiting the mind that enlightenment is possible. To reach enlightenment, the Zen Buddhist uses, among other techniques, the "koan," an absurd dialogue, question and answer, or anecdote that attempts to teach indirectly by "bypassing the mind." The classic meditation comes from Hakuin (1685–1768): "When both hands are clapped, a sound is produced: listen to the sound of one hand." There are about seventeen hundred of these koans, although not all are currently in use. Another koan is "Last night a wooden horse neighed and a stone man cut capers."[8] Again, the purpose is to get beyond logical thought.

Marilyn Ferguson, author of *The Aquarian Conspiracy,* described New Age philosophy as holding to the idea that all is one. She asserted, as do other New Age thinkers, that somehow we have come to the mistaken view that reality is distinct and that logical opposites are mutually exclusive. As a response to such thinking, Ravi Zacharias told the story of a discussion he had with an Eastern religious advocate who maintained that people in the West held to "either/or" but those in the East hold to "both-and." Ravi's reply was to note that even the "both-and" was stated by the advocate in terms of the "either/or." Francis Schaeffer put it this way: the battle in this current time is between antithesis and synthesis. Synthesis is the "both-and" perspective held by Western relativists from Friedrich Nietzsche (1844–1900) to the present and by followers of Eastern religion.

The root problem with New Age denials of the reality of the distinction between you and me, between me and a tree, between true and false or good and evil is the difficulty of accounting for the "reality" of the illusion of distinction. Ellis Potter was for fifteen years a Zen Buddhist monk. When he finally came to Christ, one reason was that it took "less faith" to believe in Christ than to believe in the Buddhist way of viewing the world. As a Buddhist, he was required to double-think on all of reality: it seemed to be so real, but he was told to believe it was not. It was a relief for Ellis to embrace this real distinct world created by God.

Os Guinness told the story of a Buddhist man who lost five sons, one after the other. Imagine the grief and pain he must have felt. Yet his Buddhism encouraged him to view the world as insubstantial and unreal like the dew that covers the ground in the morning but quickly disappears as the sun comes up. He was supposed to put to death any desire or attachment that was the source of the grief and pain. This man wrote a short poem about the tension between his Buddhism and his pain.

The world is dew
The world is dew
And yet . . . and yet[9]

Sai Baba, the guru of all gurus in India, has widespread respect in Hinduism. He has a favorite saying that also illustrates this tension between theory and reality. Sai Baba says, "Rebuked by his wife for not shedding a tear over the death of their only son, the man said, 'Last night I had a dream in which I had seven sons; when I woke, the dream vanished. Who shall I weep for, the seven who are vapor or the one that is dust? The seven were a dream, the one, a day-dream.' "[10]

The denial of distinct reality leads to the denial of grief and pain.

Christian Science also denies the reality of evil, pain and suffering as well as the reality of matter. Christian Science holds that all is God; God is good; therefore, all is good. One difficult question for the Christian Scientist is "How do you account for the 'reality' of the illusion of evil, pain and suffering?" In other words, is the illusion of evil, pain and suffering good or evil? If it is evil, then it cannot be said that all is good. If it is good, then there is no problem to be overcome by Christian Science—so who needs Christian Science? A leading Christian Science teacher admitted that he did not have an answer for this question. In a similar way, the difficulty for those in the New Age is "How do you account for the 'reality' of the illusion?"

This denial of distinct reality and the law of noncontradiction leaves Eastern religious advocates with a profound problem. Some gurus ignore the question. Other gurus say it should not be asked. Still others say the answer is *lila* (play).[11] In other words, somehow there has been an imbalance in the life force, a kind of divine play (we could even use the word *insanity*) that has produced this world of distinction. Imagine a stone being thrown into a pond and concentric ripples proceeding outward from the point of impact. The ripples are the illusion of distinct reality in the midst of the One. Would not the illusion of distinction then be the divine or the force deceiving itself? In some areas of India the insane are exalted or revered. If "sane" people believe in the "illusion" of reality, perhaps insane people who believe in what we term hallucinations are closer to reality than the sane.

Hindu philosopher Sarvepalli Radhakrishnan (1888–1975), an Oxford professor and president of India, pursued another option. When facing the issue of the seeming reality of the distinct world and the all-is-one philosophy, he said that the world is distinct and the world is one. "We do not know and cannot know why. It is all a contradiction and yet it is actual."[12] He rejected logical thinking in order to maintain his view, yet agonized over the necessity of doing so.

Any view, Eastern or Western, that maintains reality is contradictory has a profound problem, not only theoretically but practically living in the world.

REALITY IS NONCONTRADICTORY IN SOME AREAS AND CONTRADICTORY IN OTHERS

This third view of reality is not explicitly held or defended by anyone I know in the world at present, but it is the implied view of many relativists. This view assumes (or at least does not question) that reality is noncontradictory in math, science and technology but somehow assumes that reality is contradictory in religion and ethics, making it possible to view all religious and ethical views as equally true.

This strange hybrid rightly maintains that, in math and economics, 2 + 2 = 4, not 5. The proponents of this view would also readily accept science's second law of thermodynamics (entropy tends to increase), as demonstrated in every part of the known universe. They have no problem recognizing that the law of gravity is merciless and is defied at the peril of life.

In the realm of technology the law of noncontradiction is especially evident. You do not drive a normal car with only three wheels; you do not fly a plane with only one wing; you cannot drive a car from Washington, D.C., to Pittsburgh without gas in the tank. Technology also assumes that a mechanical or electrical problems can be known and fixed. Even those from Eastern religious views use airplanes, drive cars and fix equipment.

So this third view of reality accepts noncontradiction in math, science and technology, but the areas of religion and ethics are another story. Here contradiction rules. As in the second view, whatever is true for me is true for me, and whatever is true for you is true for you. Similarly, whatever is good for me is good for me alone, and whatever is good for you is good for you alone. Therefore, all religions are equally true and good. A frequent analogy that is used to explicate this view is that of a mountain with many paths reaching the top. The problem with the analogy is that it fails to acknowledge mutually exclusive views among religions on, as Steve Turner put it, "creation, heaven, hell, God, and salvation."

We examined this to some extent earlier, but figure 12.1 gives another example.

Religion	Picture	Goal
Hindu	Drop in ocean	Absorption
Buddhist	Candle and flame	Extinction
Christian	Prodigal son	Restored relationship

Figure 12.1. Three views of reality

The goal for Hinduism (*Shankara*) is transcending this world of distinction and merging with the One as a drop of water is absorbed into the ocean. The goal of Buddhism (*Theravada*) is extinguishing desire as you might blow out the flame of a candle. (In Sanskrit the word *Nirvana* comes from a root word meaning "to be extinguished" or "to be blown out.") Since in this view there is no self, then there is no self to exist after death. In contrast, believers in Christ have held that the human problem is a broken relationship with God, and its solution is reconciliation with God through Christ. This restored relationship is then enjoyed in the present life and for all eternity. The story of the prodigal son illustrates this restoration.

These starkly different views reveal a major problem with the many-paths-lead-to-the-top-of-the-mountain analogy: how could the goal of life be simultaneously or equally absorption *and* restored relationship, or extinction *and* restored relationship? Admittedly, absorption and extinction are not much different from each other—both mean a loss of individuality. However, both are poles apart from restored relationship, with its emphasis on real individuals in close, personal, loving relationships with God and others.

The problem is evident in ethics as well. How can opposite ethical views be equally valid? Can we say that the Holocaust is merely a matter of sentiment? Can the Holocaust be bad for me but good for you? Can rape be merely a matter of personal preference? Is prohibiting murder merely a cultural convention meant to preserve society, or is murder really evil? We will explore this issue in the next chapter.

This strange double-truth idea has only rarely been held in the history of philosophy. Debates between Thomas Aquinas and Averroës and Siger of Brabant raised some of these issues.[13] But could something be true in philosophy and false in theology? Could something be "formally" true and "materially" false? We could think of things like unicorns that are not philosophically or logically contradictory but that do not exist in reality. Unicorns are formally true (noncontradictory) and materially false. However, could something be materially true and formally false? In other words, does something exist in reality that is formally contradictory? If so, what is it?

⁂

BILL: *I think that all religions are saying the same thing. We need to value diversity and be multicultural. Whatever is true is true for you.*

JOHN: *I certainly value diversity and love interacting with people from other cultures, but how can you say all religions are the same? Do you think that atheism, which says there is no God, and theism, which says there is a God, are saying the same thing? Can they both be true? What about Eastern reli-*

gions, which say everything is God, and Judaism, which says there is a God dis-tinct from creation? Are they saying the same thing? Can they both be true?

BILL: *I suppose I'm saying that you can get to God (if there is one) no matter what road you take.*

JOHN: *Are you, then, saying that atheism and postmodernism are false in their denial of belief in God? Are you also saying faith in Christ is true in say-ing that a real obstacle—sin—prevents us from getting to God; and with East-ern religions that there is no sin, no distinction between good and evil, no moral problem to be overcome?*

BILL: *I guess I did not think about it that way. Perhaps, though, we don't have to use logic as you do.*

JOHN: *You live as if math, science and technology are rational. How can you say 2 + 2 = 4, the law of gravity is true and cars need gas to run and yet exempt all moral and religious views from rational consideration?*

BILL: *I just do.*

JOHN: *You might want to believe this because it makes life easier, it keeps you from conflict and you don't have to think hard about reality or God. You seem to be saying that what I would call second things (math, science and technol-ogy) matter and can be known, but first things (religion and ethics) don't mat-ter and can't be known. Second things are matters of truth but first things are merely matters of taste. Are first things no more important than whether you like chocolate or vanilla ice cream? If so, why?*

෧෨෧

In any case, this third view seems to require a justification for its claims. Can reality be contradictory in religion and ethics? Can each directly op-posite religious view be true? The difficulties with this view are many and significant, and yet many in our culture hold this view uncritically. We need to ask how or on what basis its adherents maintain that all religious or ethical views are the same or equal when they are so obviously contradictory. If they have contradictory views of reality, how can they all be true? To give one final instance, Muslims deny that Jesus died on the cross and Christians say he *did* die on the cross. Can these mutually contradictory views both be true? Is this a matter of truth or taste?

In the case of Muslim versus Christian claims about Jesus' death on the cross, historical evidence can be introduced to settle the dispute. Likewise, facts can be introduced into the argument over the true nature of reality. Facts have a way of clarifying matters, that is, they turn a discussion of abstract concepts into a discussion about concrete events—specifically, events that can be evaluated as historical or nonhistorical. Then we can further ask about the significance of these events and whether they are true or false, good or evil.

We now turn to the matter of good and evil.

13 No Room for Evil

BILL: *Well, what about the problem of evil? Doesn't that disprove Christianity?*

JOHN: *I think there are some solid intellectual answers to the problem of evil that show Christianity is not logically inconsistent at the core. But let's talk about that another time. Right now I want to point out that every world-view has a problem of evil. Your relativism has a greater problem of evil than Christianity.*

BILL: *I've never heard that before. How?*

JOHN: *Because you have no solid foundation to call anything evil. Yet there is something in our heart and conscience that screams otherwise.*

If there are no absolutes, then we cannot say anything really is evil or, for that matter, good. The problem is, we know better.

G. K. Chesterton once said, "People have given up on the idea of original sin when it's the only doctrine of Christianity that can be empirically proven." Look at the murderous reigns of Hitler and Stalin, the killing fields of Cambodia, "ethnic cleansing" in Bosnia, the stealing of food from starving people in Somalia, terrorist attacks such as those on September 11, 2001, and the crime that ravages our streets every day. Looking at these events, can we really say, "There is no evil"?

The difficult question often asked is, why does an all-good, all-powerful God allow evil? Christian theologians have wrestled with this question with no little success. I wish to point out, however, that the reality of evil serves to provide a strong argument for God's existence.

Before C. S. Lewis became a believer, it was his intellectual struggle with the problem of evil that prevented him from listening to the claims of Christ. "If a good God made the world," he asserted, "why has it gone wrong?" He refused to listen to Christian replies, supposing that such arguments were merely an attempt to avoid the obvious. Was not the universe cruel and unjust? In Lewis's opinion Lucretius had stated the problem well. "Had God designed the world it would not be a world so frail and faulty as we see."[1] Lewis called this the "argument from undesign."

It gradually dawned on Lewis, however, that he had no basis in his atheism for the idea of justice or injustice. He said,

> But how had I got this idea of just and unjust? A man does not call a line crooked unless he has some idea of a straight line. What was I comparing this universe with when I called it unjust? If the whole show was bad and senseless from A to Z, so to speak, why did I, who was supposed to be part of the show, find myself in such violent reaction against it? A man feels wet when he falls into water because man is not a water animal: a fish would not feel wet. Of course I could have given up my idea of justice by saying it was nothing but a private idea of my own. But if I did that, then my argument against God collapsed too—for the argument depended on saying that the world was really unjust, not simply that it did not happen to please my private fancies. Thus in trying to prove that God did not exist—in other words, that the whole of reality was senseless—I was forced to assume that one part of reality— namely my idea of justice was full of sense. Consequently atheism turns out to be too simple.[2]

If there is evil, Lewis concluded, there must be a fixed, absolute, "outside this world" standard by which we can know it to be really evil. If there is real evil, then we must have a fixed standard of good by which we judge it to be evil. This absolute standard of goodness suggests a God who is himself this absolute, infinite standard.

Throughout history, in fact, there has never been anything like a totally different morality where, in every case, "good" is "evil" and "evil" is "good." Lewis documented this in the appendix of *The Abolition of Man*, using illustrations from ancient Egyptians, Babylonians, Hindus, Chinese, Greeks, Romans and others. What would a totally different morality look like? Lewis wrote:

> Think of a country where people were admired for running away in
> battle, or where a man felt proud of double crossing all the people
> who had been kindest to him. You might just as well try to imagine
> a country where two and two made five. Men have differed as re-
> gards what people you ought to be unselfish to—whether it was
> only your own family, or your fellow countrymen, or everyone. But
> they have always agreed that you ought not to put yourself first.
> Selfishness has never been admired. Men have differed as to
> whether you should have one wife or four. But they have always
> agreed that you must not simply have any woman you liked.[3]

In Romans 1:29-32 the apostle Paul gave a long list of evils he assumed everyone knows:

> being filled with all unrighteousness, wickedness, greed, evil; full
> of envy, murder, strife, deceit, malice; they are gossips, slanderers,
> haters of God, insolent, arrogant, boastful, inventors of evil, dis-
> obedient to parents, without understanding, untrustworthy, un-
> loving, unmerciful; and although they *know the ordinance of God,*
> that those who practice *such things* are worthy of death, they not
> only do the same, but also give hearty approval to those who prac-
> tice them. (emphasis added)

Paul contended that each of the evils in this list is, in fact, known by all people. He described this law as "written in their hearts," or on their consciences (Rom 2:15). This conscious awareness of the law can be dulled or perhaps (in the case of a sociopath) lost, but it is usually retained to some degree even in the most calloused people. Even totalitarian dictators or terrorists show care for their own families and have friendships with some people around them. The so-called Mob has its own code of behavior toward those of its own inner circle, even though this code may not apply to those outside.

There seems to be a universal agreement on first principles with some disagreement on secondary issues. If there is real evil, then there must be an absolute standard by which it can be judged to be so. If there is injustice, there must be a standard of justice. The alternatives are these: (1) to make all moral statements meaningless and absurd, or (2) to reduce them to arbitrary personal preference, thus making statements about "evil" mere matters of sentiment.

THE CULTURAL MOVE

Some try to avoid this impasse by attempting to construct an ethic based on that which is good for society. They reason that it is possible to get a sufficient number of people to agree to a "categorical imperative" (said Immanuel Kant, 1724–1804) to do only that which we would will to become a universal standard. Others suggest that we could make it our goal to be impartial, standing behind a "veil of ignorance" (said John Rawls), so that our bias does not distract. *Then* we can construct a basis for social ethics.

Murder, for example. We might begin by arguing that outlawing murder would be in the interest of preserving society. This is undoubtedly true. If people regularly killed other people, society would be chaotic and unsafe. If murder were practiced on a large scale, it would soon deplete the numbers of people in that society. Outlawing murder *will* preserve society.

However, some could question whether our society *ought* to be preserved. Terrorists, for example, want to destroy the United States no matter how many people are killed. On what basis, then, ought the U.S.

to be protected? And what do you say to those who reject the "categorical imperative" or the "veil of ignorance"? Is murder intrinsically wrong? If so, it is evil and must have an absolute standard by which it is judged to be so. Is the prohibition of murder only in the pragmatic interest of the culture, and is it wrong merely because it is supported by the majority of that society? If so, then we can say, "We are the majority. We say murder is wrong. If you murder, we will arrest you and put you in jail. Might makes right." In this case murder is wrong only because the majority says so. You have gathered a sufficient group around this law (or any other law) to gain its approval.

The reason that such attempts can never work is principial. You cannot get "ought" out of "is." On this point Lewis argued,

> From propositions about fact alone no practical conclusion can ever be drawn. *This will preserve society* cannot lead to *do this* except by the mediation of *society ought to be preserved. This will cost you your life* cannot lead directly to *do not do this:* it can lead to it only through a felt desire or an acknowledged duty of self-preservation. The Innovator is trying to get a conclusion in the *imperative mood* out of premises in the *indicative mood;* and though he continues trying to all eternity, he cannot succeed for the thing is impossible.[4]

In a discussion over a moral question, charges may be made: "Who are you to try to impose your morality on me?" In other words, the charge is "Says who?" or "Whose morality and whose justice?" The same question could be asked by a minority challenging the majority: "Who are you, majority, to impose your morality on us?"

MAJORITY: "This will preserve society."

MINORITY: "I do not want this society preserved. I will not accept your laws."

MAJORITY: "Then we will arrest you."

MINORITY: "Again, who are you to impose your morality on me?"

MAJORITY: "Says us."

Atheist and Yale law professor Arthur Leff published a legal essay in the *Duke Law Journal* (1979) entitled "Unspeakable Ethics, Unnatural Law." It came to be considered a classic. In it he argued that there is no normative system of ethics based in anything other than the bare assertion of human will. The common cultural move will not work because of what he called "the grand sez who." Interestingly, though an atheist, he did admit that "sez God" would provide solid basis for ethics and law. He started his essay by saying,

> I want to believe—and so do you—in a complete transcendent and immanent set of propositions about right and wrong; findable rules that authoritatively, and unambiguously direct us how to live righteously. I also want to believe—and so do you—in no such thing, but rather that we are wholly free, not only to choose for ourselves what we ought to do, but decide for ourselves, individually and as a species, what we ought to be. What we want, heaven help us, is simultaneously to be perfectly ruled and perfectly free, that is, at the same time to discover the right and the good and to create it. . . . My plan for this article, then, is as follows. I shall try to prove to your satisfaction that there cannot be any normative system ultimately based on anything except human will.[5]

Leff argued that much of the current debate on the foundation of law is rooted in this tension between "found law" and "made law." There is a corresponding tension between these two particularly because we may fear that in the end "we are able to locate nothing more attractive, or more final, than ourselves."[6] In order to find "normative propositions," we must find one that is immune from criticism—unchallengeable. Why would it be wrong to violate the command "Thou shalt not commit adultery"? To put it in other words, when would it be impermissible to put forward the schoolyard or barroom trump card—"the grand sez who"? In order to do this, we would have to find an evaluator above being evaluated. The evaluator must be "the unjudged judge, the unruled legislator, the premise maker who rests on no premises, the uncreated creator of values. Now, what would you call such a thing if it existed? You would call it Him."[7]

The reason, Leff said, I ought not commit adultery would be if and only if the speaker is God. A God-grounded system has no "analogues." If God does not exist, no one can take his place. "Anything that took his place would also be Him."[8] A statement like "you ought to do X" would be binding only if the speaker had the power to make X good. Under what circumstances can someone propose an ethical statement that withstands the cosmic "Says who?"

"There are no such circumstances . . . there is no one like the Lord," Leff continued.

> If He does not exist, there is no metaphoric equivalent. No person, no combination of people, no document however hallowed by time, no process, no premise, nothing is equivalent to an actual God in this central function as the unexaminable examiner of good and evil. The so-called death of God turns out not to have been just His funeral; it also seems to have effected the total elimination of any coherent, or even more than momentarily convincing, ethical or legal system.[9]

If law cannot be in God, Leff argued, then the only possible alternative is to say that the law is in us—one of us, some of us, all of us. We can either sing, "We're free of God," or "Oh, God, we're free." We need then to ask, who among us *ought* to be able to declare a law that ought to be obeyed? We could make each individual create his or her own law, so that each person becomes, in effect, a godlet. But then who decides the rules among these multiplicities of "gods"? If there is conflict, who ought to give way? You could set up rules that govern "inter-divinity transactions" that suggest that godlets should not use force or fraud to accomplish their ends. "What you could not do is defend it on the basis of Godlet preference."[10] The "whatever is true for me is true for me and whatever is true for you is true for you" philosophy makes evaluating any respective claims impossible.

We could try to get out of this dilemma by counting noses or by discriminating among the qualities of the "ethical boxes." Counting noses does not, however, make the result "right" and other preferences "wrong." And could we judge the quality? It seems not, because there can be no fixed or absolute standards by which we can judge good/bad or better/best when each person is his or her own godlet.

Many people have nevertheless taken this second route. They have a "considered" view or a "serious and reflective view" or have reached a "reflective equilibrium" or have an imagined "veil of ignorance." Who is to decide which position is more "considered" and who says that the more "considered" position is more ethical or right? You could start with a declaration that some basic belief is good and build from there, but then that basic belief would have to be "good" to someone. Perhaps you could gain a considerable following that agrees that this starting proposition is good, but how do we evaluate this claim? Leff went on to say, *"There is no such thing as an unchallengeable evaluative system.* There is no way to prove one ethical system superior to any other, *unless* at some point an evaluator is asserted to have the final uncontradictable, unexaminable word. That choice of unjudged judge, whoever is given the role, is itself, strictly speaking arbitrarily."[11]

In Robert Nozick's book *Anarchy, State, and Utopia,* he asserted, "Individuals have rights, and there are things no person or group may do to them [without violating their rights]."[12] This seems reasonable enough, but if individuals have rights—*says who?* Also, who decides the rules when people who have equal rights differ about what is to be done? Richard Posner put forward an ethical system in which no person may dominate any other.[13] This is great when two individuals or more decide to make this "deal" with each other. However, what if someone refuses this deal? All you can say is, "No deal." You could get a lot of people to agree on the above assumptions, but if questioned with the "grand sez who," the only final answer is "sez us."

Leff concluded the article with this statement:

> All I can say is this: it looks as if we are all we have. Given what we know about each other and ourselves, this is an extraordinarily unappetizing prospect. . . . Neither reason nor love nor terror, seems to have worked to make us "good," worse than that, there is no reason why anything should. Only if ethics were unspeakable by us could law be unnatural and unchallengeable. As things stand now, everything is up for grabs. Nevertheless:
>
> Napalming babies is bad.
> Starving the poor is wicked.
> Buying and selling each other is depraved.
> Those who stood up and died resisting Hitler, Stalin, Amin,
> Pol Pot, and
> General Custer, too, have earned salvation.
> Those who acquiesced deserve to be damned.
> There is in the world such a thing as evil.
> All together now—sez who?
> God help us![14]

Postmodernists like Richard Rorty, Stanley Fish and Alistair McIntire all understand this critique. They give up a rational basis for ethics but wrongly assume that "sez God" can equally be rejected.

☙

BILL: *I think you can have morality without God—just determine what is good for the culture.*

JOHN: *Who determines what is good, especially when there are so many differing views?*

BILL: *I think we could get a great majority of people in this culture to say murder is wrong.*

JOHN: *I certainly agree that murder is wrong, but is the only reason you say it is wrong because a majority says so? What would you say to a minority member, such as a terrorist who would want to murder as many people as possible? Or what if the majority changed their mind and said murder was right? Is murder in itself wrong or only because you say so?*

BILL: *Outlawing murder will preserve society.*

JOHN: *I agree, but you can't get "ought" out of "is" or the imperative out of the indicative. This will preserve society, but it does not necessarily mean society ought to be preserved. What do you say to someone who doesn't care for this society to be preserved—"says us"? Who are you to impose your group morality on us?*

BILL: *Well, then, why do you think murder is wrong?*

JOHN: *"Sez God."*

It is important to consider the ancient dilemma: Is something right because God says it is or does God say it because it is right? In the former case, God's will seems arbitrary (he just says it). In the latter case, it seems there is a standard higher than God (the right or good). The classic answer to this dilemma is that there is a third option: the good is rooted in the character of God himself. In fact, God's revelation of his will in Scripture is a reflection of his character and it also fits how he has made us. What God "sez" is like the owner's manual of a car. If you violate what it says, the car will not run at all or will at least not run well. God's will is our self-interest now and eternally, and is not unnecessarily restrictive.

WE NEED TO POINT OUT INCONSISTENCIES

Even though he remained an atheist, Arthur Leff provided us a brilliant critique of attempts to ground an ethical system without God. Sadly, Leff died of cancer in 1984 at age forty-eight. I wish someone had had the opportunity to move him toward an adequate basis for his highest aspirations. If there is evil, and he knew that there is, he could have been asked, "Why do you not believe in the unjudged judge, the unruled legislator, the uncreated creator of values, the unnatural law and that which is unchallengeable by the 'grand sez who'? Are there objections we could clear up? Are there some things that need to be explained? If there is evil, there must be an absolute good in order for us to judge it to be really evil. If there is an absolute good or evil, it is hard to resist the conclusion that there must be a God who is good, allowing us to say, 'Sez God.'"

If someone is not yet willing to admit that evil exists, perhaps that person could be gently moved toward the logical conclusion of his or her false assumptions. For instance, journalist Arthur Koestler interviewed a Japanese expert in Buddhism, who denied the existence of good and evil.

Koestler: You favor tolerance towards all religions and political systems. What about Hitler's gas chambers?

Buddhist: That was very silly of him.

Koestler: Just silly, not evil?

Buddhist: Evil is a Christian concept. Good and evil exist only on a relative scale.[15]

Many may not be willing to go so far. For instance, a believing friend of mine took graduate classes under Richard Rorty, a leading postmodern philosopher. In one such class he met a woman who was Jewish by heritage but was actually an atheist and a feminist. Being influenced by Rorty's teaching, she claimed there were no absolutes. My friend, knowing what she cared about, said, "I can prove to you that you believe in absolutes."

"No, you can't!"

"Yes, I can. I'll give you two: rape and the Holocaust are morally wrong."

She thought for a while and said, "You're right." Yet she had no basis on which to hold these values.

One time, in a graduate class, Rorty was talking about how the abolition of slavery was achieved. He pointed out that the cultural paradigm changed, which allowed that abolition to be possible. In other words, when a community has moral beliefs and principles that contradict a certain action, only then can that action be said to be unjust for them. My friend, who is African American, raised a question.

FRIEND: "If that paradigm had not changed, would the horrible abuses of slavery (kidnapping, harsh treatment, many deaths on slave ships, and so on) be wrong?"

RORTY: "But it did change."

FRIEND: "But if it did not, would it be wrong?"

RORTY: "But it did change."

FRIEND: "But what if it did not?"

RORTY: "If the community held no belief inconsistent with it, I don't think we could call it unjust for them."

FRIEND (with passion): "That is unacceptable!"

Rorty said that was the best he could offer. The classroom fell into silence. A number of students came up after class and thanked my friend for asking the question. In this case Rorty finally answered the question. In other situations his stated policy is to ignore or evade. He advocates that you should not "play the game" by others' rules. Once a student of mine asked Rorty in a public setting about how his postmodern pragmatism dealt with the Holocaust. He abruptly responded, "I don't answer that kind of question anymore."

In Rorty's published writings he does, however, answer the question of the Holocaust more directly. In a classic autobiographical essay,

"Trotsky and Wild Orchids," Rorty complained that his view "is often referred to dismissively as 'cultural relativism.' "

> But it is not relativistic if that means saying that every moral view is as good as every other. Our moral view is *I firmly believe, much better* than any compelling view, even though there are many people to whom you will never be able to convert to it. It is one thing to say, falsely, that there is nothing to choose between the Nazis and us. It is another thing to say, correctly, that there is no neutral, common ground to which a philosophical Nazi and I can repair to argue out our differences.[16]

If there is "no neutral, common ground" to settle the debate with the Nazis, then why is Rorty's view "much better"? It would seem that it is better because he "firmly believes" that it is—"sez Rorty" or "sez Rorty's community." In an essay in the *Human Rights Reader*, Rorty suggested that the basis for human rights is not rationality or moral law but "what Baier calls 'a progress of sentiments.' . . . It is the result of what I have been calling 'sentimental education.' "[17]

So the basis for morality, in Rorty's view, is "sentiment." We are back to preferences and tastes. But whose sentiments? Rorty's? A Nazi's? Or someone else's? Since morality is not based on a neutral ground, it is merely a matter of arbitrary personal preference. Many might (rightly) agree with Rorty's sentiments contra Nazism, but what if someone holds the opposite sentiments? How do we decide between them? I quite agree that we need an education of sentiments, but in the absence of a standard of justice or good, we would not know which sentiments to choose. I would suggest that Rorty's conscience is better than his philosophy at this point.

James Miller, an author sympathetic to postmodernism, wrote *The Passion of Michel Foucault,* in which he argued that many of Foucault's American followers (Rorty included) put a rather attractive face on Foucault's radical version of postmodern philosophy:

Most of these latter-day American Foucaultians are high-minded democrats; they are committed to forging a more diverse society in which whites and people of color, straights and gays, men and women, their various ethnic and gender differences intact, can nevertheless all live together in compassionate harmony—an appealing if difficult goal, with deep roots in the Judeo-Christian tradition.[18]

Notice that this postmodern vision (à la Rorty's respect for kindness) had deep, though unacknowledged, roots in the Judeo-Christian tradition. You can almost hear Christ's "love your neighbor" or Paul's there is "no Jew nor Greek, slave nor free, male nor female." Miller admitted, though, that Foucault's work is "far more unconventional" and disturbing. Foucault, more consistently, wanted to destroy everything that is claimed to be "right" by Western culture. Miller noted as well that Foucault's destruction targets extended to "nearly everything that passes for 'right' among a great many of America's left-wing academics."[19]

Foucault wanted to maintain that there are no limits, no divisions, no boundaries between good and evil, reason and unreason, subject and object. Much more radical than other postmodernists, Foucault focused often on the motto "Be cruel" and on images of torture and death.

Foucault expressed this boundary smashing especially in his views of sexuality. Foucault pursued his philosophy in practice, engaging in sadomasochism and in anonymous gay sex in San Francisco bathhouses. He contracted AIDS and died in 1985 as a result. Miller titled one chapter in his biography "Be Cruel." Miller's interest in writing this biography was provoked by rumors that Foucault had deliberately infected others with AIDS. He found this suggestion troubling and searched for answer to this charge throughout his book. Fortunately, he found no evidence to verify these rumors. What I find interesting is that Miller and others would be so troubled by this, if it were the case, given Foucault's stated philosophy.

Foucault definitely shows us a darker, more Nietzschean side of relativism that pushes beyond limits that even most relativists find abhorrent. We might ask relativists what stops them from advocating the worst atrocities.

NEW AGE

Earlier, we noted that New Age beliefs hold reality to be contradictory, or "nondual," in accordance with the principle of nondistinction. If all is one, then there are no real distinctions in the world and all apparent distinctions are illusory, a state or condition called *Maya*. This leads to the conclusion that matter, time and space, and the distinctions between true and false, good and evil, are illusory as well.

Most people do not realize how pervasive this denial of the reality of "good" and "evil" is in Eastern religion. The following are some examples.

Mythologist Joseph Campbell (1904–1987), in a PBS interview with Bill Moyers, called good and evil mere "apparitions of temporality." Struggling with the implications of this idea, Campbell went to a Hindu guru and asked him whether we must say yes or no to things normally considered evil, things like brutality and vulgarity. The guru thought about it and responded, "For you and me, we must say 'yes.' "

Rajneesh, who had a considerable following nationally and internationally, said, "We have divided the world into the good and the evil. The world is not so divided. The good and evil are our valuations. . . . Valuation is human. It is our imposition, it is our projection. . . . There is no good; there is no bad. . . . So, do not impose on the creative process (God) your own feelings, your own valuations; rather, if you want to know the Creator, Creative Process, go beyond these dualisms."[20]

Zen master Yun-Men once said, "I want you to get the plain truth; be not concerned with right and wrong; the conflict between right and wrong is sickness of the mind."[21]

Herman Hesse, in his rendering of the life of Buddha, *Siddhartha,* said, "The world . . . is not imperfect or slowly evolving along a path to perfection. No, it is perfect at every moment. . . . Therefore, it seems to me that everything that exists is good—death as well as life, sin as well as holiness, wisdom as well as folly."[22]

I have personally met many New Age leaders who would agree with this view theoretically but who, I am convinced, would not dream of applying it practically in sinister, malicious or cruel acts. Nor do I think the authors mentioned here would torture people. However, it is important to underline that there would be no reason, based on their views, to prohibit such cruelty from being practiced. The principle of nondistinction that makes it difficult for those in the New Age to talk about that which is true or false also makes it difficult, if not impossible, to speak of good and evil.

NEOPAGANISM

At a meeting of neopagans, the participants put together "13 Principles." One was "We do not accept the concept of 'absolute evil' nor do we worship any entity known as 'Satan' or the 'Devil.' "[23] In their view Satanism is a Christian heresy because it involves inverting and rebelling against the biblical God and therefore assumes the biblical worldview—a worldview they reject. Not only do they reject the "absolute evil" of Satan, but they also reject any distinction between good and evil. Erica Jong said, "Satanists . . . accept the duality between good and evil; pagans do not. . . . Pagans see good and evil as allied, in fact, indivisible."[24]

Another neopagan advocate, Starhawk, said of the goddess: "The nature of the Goddess is never single. . . . She is light and darkness, the patroness of love and death, who makes all possibilities. She brings forth comfort and pain. . . . As Crone, she is the dark face of life that demands death and sacrifice. . . . In Witchcraft, the dark waning aspect of the God is not evil—it is a vital part of the natural structure."[25]

One of the predecessors of neopaganism, Alistair Crowley, said in 1903 that the only rule of witchcraft was "Do what thou wilt shall be the whole of the Law."[26] This has continued to be the Wiccan "Rede," or rule for living, with only one addition: "Harm none and do as you will." While I am glad that "harm none" was added, it begs the question "Is harming really evil and not harming really good?" "Harm none" sounds curiously like a negative way of saying, "Love your neighbor"—the Golden Rule.

WHICH IS TRUE OR GOOD?

If atheism, postmodernism, pantheism and neopaganism agree on anything, it is that there are no absolutes, no fixed points, no ultimate basis from which to talk about real good and real evil. The existence of real evil would, in fact, make each of these worldviews false, because none has a means to account for evil. If there is no such thing as good or evil, then Judaism, Islam and Christianity are all false. And though relativists would be loath to make such a statement, it must be said: one view must be wrong and one must be right. You cannot have it both ways.

☙

BILL: *All you have shown me is that unless God exists, it is difficult, if not impossible, to have objective moral values.*

JOHN: *If I have convinced you of that, then I have made much progress. In fact, I would take what you agree to a step further. I would say:*

- *Unless God exists, there is no objective evil (or good).*
- *There is evil (and good).*
- *Therefore, God exists.*

BILL: *Slow down! I don't agree.*

JOHN: *Which one of the two premises is false?*

BILL: *I don't know. After what you have shared with me, both seem true, but I don't like your conclusion.*

JOHN: *Well, let's keep talking. Would you like to meet next week?*

BILL: *OK. I have enjoyed our conversations. It is good to talk to someone like you, who doesn't get paranoid and take it personally if I make strong objections. Let's keep talking.*

TRUTH THAT TRANSFORMS

Throughout this book we have seen the outlines of a way to address the issue of truth at the beginning of the twenty-first century. We need to uphold absolutes without absolutism, practice rationality without rationalism, make assertions without arrogance and offer a defense without defensiveness. In doing so, we need three priorities: right thinking, right practice and right attitudes. Even when the first two are clearly maintained, the third is sometimes lacking. The defense of the gospel is most effective when combined with the demeanor of Christ.

Relativism has massive negative consequences for our lives; it is self-contradictory, confuses truth with taste, provides no basis for real evil and is, in practice, hopelessly inconsistent. Although relativists charge those who believe in absolutes with arrogance, we have seen that it is the dogmatic relativist who claims (implicitly) to possess infinite knowledge. On the other hand, we have seen that believers not only can proclaim absolutes without absolutism but that this approach is based on Scripture. Although we claim knowledge of the revelation of Christ, we are finite people who confront fallen situations. Far from being know-it-alls and having "black and white" knowledge of everything, we face difficult decisions when we attempt to relate truth to the complexities of life.

Believers not only have a solid base for tolerance, but our tolerance is also rooted in the love of Christ. Even when we are right, we are not thereby righteous. We can assert without arrogance, give a defense without defensiveness and have solid grounds for rejecting absolutism whether inside or outside the church.

OUR URGENT NEED

The age in which we live needs to recapture God's truth—a truth that transforms, a truth that renews, a truth that reforms, a truth set on fire by the Holy Spirit. We need a truth that is decisive for our thinking, worship and action. All too often we see that the truth "has stumbled in the street" (Is 59:14). Smoldering embers need to be fanned and fuel added so that a roaring fire might warm our families, churches and every area of public life.

In many ways this inability to see truth or affirm it is related not primarily to intellectual issues but is a matter of the imagination, the heart and ultimately the will. As long as truth is held to be unclear, it lacks any binding force in our lives. It is convenient to question objectivity, raise issues about words and reject moral absolutes because it leaves us free to do what we want. The more highly we regard ourselves, the less we want to receive truth from anybody. The more humble we are, the more open we are to receiving truth wherever we find it.

The question is whether any religious belief can lay claim to being "true truth." Faith in Christ is that truth or it is a false belief. Either faith in Christ is true, historically grounded and decisive for our lives or it is false and there is another way—or perhaps no way. If it is true, it has ultimate significance; if it is not true, it is a mere curio piece fit for a museum. The one thing it cannot be is a matter of taste.

THE CHURCH

People in the church don't want to maintain "true truth" because of desires for academic respectability, doubt arising from secular education, the unpopularity of absolutes in the culture and perhaps an uneasy feeling that the more we acknowledge truth, the more accountable we are. At the same time, we suffer from a pride that causes us to not want to look in a mirror and see ourselves as we really are. What we need is a spiritual wisdom given by the Holy Spirit that both humbles and enlightens, enabling us to see with new clarity.

We need to recover truth, mobilizing and calling our churches to teach it, equipping seminaries to see its importance, appealing to the culture to see the truth that is there, right before their eyes, and pleading with believers not to exchange their inheritance for a mess of pottage. This does not involve a return to the past per se, although there is much to learn from those who have gone before us. We need to train tomorrow's leaders to understand the crisis of our times and see the opportunities before them.

The church is so divided over how to confront the culture that we need much more interaction among people of differing opinions to find common ground. Perhaps groups with common concerns can link together on this issue of truth so that they can be much stronger together than they could be individually. The goal would be a united call to hold up Christ as the true, the good and the beautiful and to view the world from that vantage point. C. S. Lewis said that he believed in Christ as he believed that the sun is risen, not because he saw it clearly, but because by it he saw everything else.[1]

We need outstanding believers in each profession to write books in their disciplines with their faith implicit and with their scholarship impeccable. They need to lay out the truth in their discipline as well as the ambiguities, the danger of bias, prejudice or subjectivity to which people in their discipline are liable. They need to approach the truth fearlessly with the belief that all truth is God's truth. They can learn everything they can about anything they can because each particular truth points to the God of truth. After all, we come to believe in something not just when something proves it but only when everything proves it.

May the Lord use these words to stir others to go further and deeper. Lord, give us your Spirit so we can see. Without you, everything is vague and unfocused. Lord, give us your clarity so we can discern the times before us. Help us, like the noble Bereans, to sift truth from error. May God raise up new leaders to take on the task of holding truth up as a torch. May this book honor our Lord. Soli Deo Gloria.

NOTES

Chapter 1: What Is Truth?

[1]In the United States, the number of people who believe in God has consistently been in the ninetieth percentile.

[2]The polls, ranging from two-thirds to eight-tenths of people polled, say that there are no absolutes. A Barna poll taken February 12, 2002, for example, has 64 percent believing that truth is always relative. For the latest polling data, go to <www.barna.org>.

[3]One poll shows that 54 percent of those claiming to be born again denied believing in absolutes. For more information go to <www.barna.org>.

[4]See Sarah Hinlickly, "Talking to Generation X," *First Things* 90 (February 1999).

[5]C. S. Lewis, *The Latin Letters of C. S. Lewis: The Correspondence of C. S. Lewis and Don Giovanni Calabria*, trans. and ed. Martin Moynihan (Ann Arbor, Mich.: Servant, 1988), p. 89.

[6]Peter Kreeft has one of his dialogue characters (who seems to represent Kreeft's view) say, "There are different kinds of relativism: . . . metaphysical relativism, epistemological relativism, moral relativism, and religious relativism. You can claim that there are no absolutes anywhere in reality—that is metaphysical relativism. Or anywhere in religion—that is religious relativism" (*A Refutation of Moral Relativism: Interviews with an Absolutist* [San Francisco: Ignatius Press, 1999], p. 28). For the six major families of postmodernism see D. A. Carson, *The Gagging of God: Christianity Confronts Pluralism* (Grand Rapids, Mich.: Zondervan, 1996), pp. 78-79 n. 66. To summarize: (1) Hermeneutical philosophy—Gadamer and Ricoeur, (2) later Wittgenstein, (3) philosophy of science—Polanyi, Kuhn and Toulmin, (4) neo-Reformed—Plantinga and Wolterstorff, (5) French post-structuralism—Derrida, Foucault and Lyotard, and (6) American neopragmatism—Rorty, Stout and Cornel West.

[7]See my recommended book list at the end of this book.

[8]See discussions of various views on truth in Douglas Groothuis, *Truth Decay: Defending Christianity Against the Challenges of Postmodernism* (Downers Grove, Ill.: InterVarsity Press, 2000), esp. chaps. 3 and 4, and in James Emery White, *What Is Truth? A Comparative Study of the Positions of Cornelius Van Til, Francis Schaeffer, Carl F. H. Henry, Donald Bloesch, Millard Erickson* (Nashville: Broadman & Holman, 1994).

Chapter 2: True Tolerance

[1] I am indebted for this last thought and the previous paragraph to the work of Os Guinness. He expressed these ideas in lectures at Cedar Point Farm, "The Williamsburg Charter," and his book *The American Hour: A Time of Reckoning and the Once and Future Role of Faith* (New York: Free Press, 1993).

[2] Lesslie Newbigin, *The Open Secret: Sketches for a Missionary Theology* (Grand Rapids, Mich.: Eerdmans, 1978), p. 124.

[3] T. W. Manson, *Sayings of Jesus* (London: SCM Press, 1937), p. 261.

[4] Quoted in Kenneth Bailey, *Poet and Peasant and Through Peasant Eyes: A Literary-Cultural Approach to the Parables in Luke* (Grand Rapids, Mich.: Eerdmans, 1976), p. 40.

[5] See the discussion of the multicultural nature of Christianity in John Piper, *Let the Nations Be Glad! The Supremacy of God in Missions,* 2nd ed. (Grand Rapids, Mich.: Baker Academic, 2003).

[6] Some helpful books on tolerance are the following: Stan Gaede, *When Tolerance Is No Virtue* (Downers Grove, Ill.: InterVarsity Press, 1993); and Josh McDowell, *The New Tolerance* (Wheaton, Ill.: Tyndale House, 1998).

[7] Francis Beckwith, "Liberal Tolerance," *Christian Research Journal* 22, no. 3:46.

[8] Dorothy L. Sayers, "The Pantheon Papers," in *The Whimsical Christian: 18 Essays* (New York: Collier, 1987), p. 4.

[9] Dorothy L. Sayers, "The Other Six Deadly Sins," in *Whimsical Christian,* p. 176.

[10] Os Guinness, from lectures at Cedar Point Farm. This theme is also found in Os Guinness, *The East, No Exit* (Downers Grove, Ill.: InterVarsity Press, 1974), p. 50.

[11] Ibid., p. 50.

[12] Alister E. McGrath, *Passion for Truth: The Intellectual Coherence of Evangelicalism* (Downers Grove, Ill.: InterVarsity Press, 1996), p. 219.

[13] Ibid., p. 239.

Chapter 3: Right, Not Righteous

[1] Kenneth Bailey, *Poet and Peasant and Through Peasant Eyes: A Literary-Cultural Approach to the Parables in Luke* (Grand Rapids, Mich.: Eerdmans, 1976), pp. 78–79.

[2] Ibid., p. 79.

[3] See R. C. Sproul and Art Lindsley, "Twenty Years After the Death of God Movement," *Christianity Today,* June 14, 1985, pp. 19–20, quoting William Hamilton, whom I interviewed for the article.

[4] Bailey, *Poet and Peasant and Through Peasant Eyes,* p. 80.

[5] William Fenner, *The Works of William Fenner* (London: E. Tyler for I. Stafford,

1657), pp. 108ff.

[6]Hillel (Mishna Pirke, Aboth 2:5), cited in Bailey, *Poet and Peasant and Through Peasant Eyes,* p. 149.

[7]Joachim Jeremias, *The Parables of Jesus,* trans. S. H. Hooke, rev. ed. (London: SCM Press, 1963), p. 114, cited in Bailey, *Poet and Peasant and Through Peasant Eyes,* p. 156.

Chapter 4: Assertions Without Arrogance

[1]Martin Luther, quoted in "Martin Luther: The Early Years," *Christian History* 11, no. 2 (1992): 27.

[2]Martin Luther, *The Bondage of the Will,* trans. Henry Cole (Grand Rapids, Mich.: Eerdmans, 1931), p. 24.

[3]Martin Luther, quoted in J. H. Merle D'Aubigne, *The Life and Times of Martin Luther* (Chicago: Moody Press, 1978), pp. 207–8.

[4]Martin Luther, quoted in *Christian History* 11, no. 2 (1992): 50. Luther's last sentence was included in the first printed version of the events but was not recorded on the spot.

[5]John Calvin, *Institutes of the Christian Religion,* ed. John T. McNeill, trans. Ford Lewis Battles (Philadelphia: Westminster Press, 1960), 2:2:15, emphasis added.

[6]John Calvin, *Genesis Commentary* (Grand Rapids, Mich.: Eerdmans, 1963), 1:217–18, emphasis added.

[7]I am indebted to Dr. Bruce Waltke for this line of thought, developed in lectures on Proverbs at Cedar Point Farm.

Chapter 5: Infallible Absolutes, Fallible People

[1]G. K. Chesterton, *As I Was Saying: A Chesterton Reader,* ed. Robert Knille (Grand Rapids, Mich.: Eerdmans, 1985), p. 270.

[2]Benjamin B. Warfield, *Selected Shorter Writings of Benjamin B. Warfield* (Nutley, N.J.: Presbyterian & Reformed, 1970–1973), 2:463–465.

[3]Jonathan Culler, *On Deconstruction* (Ithaca, N.Y.: Cornell University Press, 1982), p. 149. Cited in David Lehman, *Signs of the Times* (New York: Poseidon, 1991), pp. 61–62.

[4]Millard J. Erickson, *Truth or Consequences: The Promise and Perils of Postmodernism* (Downers Grove, Ill.: InterVarsity Press, 2001), p. 209. Erickson quotes Sandra Harding as claiming that relativism is "fundamentally a sexist response that attempts to preserve the legitimacy of androcentric claims in the face of contrary evidence."

[5]C. S. Lewis, "The Poison of Subjectivism," in C. S. Lewis, *Christian Reflections,* ed.

Walter Hooper (Grand Rapids, Mich.: Eerdmans, 1967), p. 77.

[6]Ibid., pp. 77–78. See also J. Budziszewski, *What We Can't Not Know* (Dallas: Spence, 2003).

[7]See Thomas C. Oden's systematic theology, particularly vol. 1, *The Living God* (San Francisco: Harper & Row, 1987), p. 13.

[8]Thomas C. Oden, *After Modernity—What? Agenda for Theology* (Grand Rapids, Mich.: Zondervan, 1992), p. 22.

Chapter 6: Infallible Absolutes, Fallen Situations

[1]Carl F. H. Henry, *A Plea for Evangelical Demonstration* (Grand Rapids, Mich.: Baker Academic, 1971).

[2]I took these four options from a talk given on tape by Francis Schaeffer.

[3]Peter Kreeft, *A Refutation of Moral Relativism: Interviews with an Absolutist* (San Francisco: Ignatius, 1999), p. 162.

Chapter 7: Defense Without Defensiveness

[1]Søren Kierkegaard, cited in R. Kent Hughes, *Luke*, vol. 2 (Wheaton, Ill.: Crossway, 1998), p. 53. No further citation is given for this quotation or the proverbial saying on worrying.

[2]Ibid.

[3]Os Guinness, "More Victimized Than Thou," in *No God but God: Breaking with the Idols of Our Age,* ed. Os Guinness and John Seel (Chicago: Moody Press, 1992), p. 86.

[4]Os Guinness, lecture at Cedar Point Farm.

[5]Martyn Lloyd-Jones, *Spiritual Depression: Its Causes and Cure* (Grand Rapids, Mich.: Eerdmans, 1965).

[6]"Prautes," in *The Hebrew-Greek Key Study Bible, NASB,* ed. Spiros Zodhiates (Chattanooga, Tenn.: AMG, 1992), note 4240, p. 1869.

[7]Guinness, "More Victimized Than Thou," p. 92.

Chapter 8: When Arguments Fail

[1]C. S. Lewis, *Letters of C. S. Lewis,* ed. W. H. Lewis (Orlando, Fla.: Harcourt Brace, 1993), p. 446.

[2]I am indebted to Os Guinness for this point and the need for an indirect approach given in a lecture at Cedar Point Farm.

[3]C. S. Lewis, *Mere Christianity* (New York: Touchstone, 1996), pp. 124–25.

[4]Charles Colson, from the tape series *Why Believe*, tape 5, side A: "Is There Truth?"

[5]Dorothy L. Sayers, *The Whimsical Christian: 18 Essays* (New York: Collier, 1987), pp. 13–14.

[6]Ibid., pp. 15–16.

[7]Ibid., p. 24.

[8]Ibid., pp. 27–28.

[9]C. S. Lewis, "Bluspels and Flalansferes," in C. S. Lewis, *Selected Literary Essays*, ed. Walter Hooper (Cambridge: Cambridge University Press, 1969), p. 265.

[10]C. S. Lewis, "Weight of Glory," in C. S. Lewis, *Weight of Glory and Other Literary Addresses* (San Francisco: HarperCollins, 1976), p. 26.

[11]C. S. Lewis, *Surprised by Joy: The Shape of My Early Life* (New York: Harcourt Brace, 1956), p. 181.

[12]Ibid.

[13]Michael Novak, "Skirmish in the Culture War," *Crisis* 11, no. 3 (1993): 7.

Chapter 9: Absolutists in Disguise?

[1]Charles Griswold, quoted in David Lehman, *Signs of the Times: Deconstruction and the Fall of Paul de Man* (New York: Poseidon, 1991), pp. 224–25.

[2]Jacques Derrida, "Force of Law: The Mystical Foundation of Authority," in *Deconstruction and the Possibility of Justice*, ed. Drucilla Cornell, Michel Rosenfeld and David Gray Carlson (New York: Routledge, 1992), pp. 14–15.

[3]C. S. Lewis, *The Abolition of Man; or, Reflections on Education with Special Reference to the Teaching of English in the Upper Forms of School* (Oxford: Collier, 1947), pp. 40–41.

[4]Francis Schaeffer, *The God Who Is There: Speaking Historic Christianity into the Twentieth Century* (Downers Grove, Ill.: InterVarsity Press, 1968), p. 101.

[5]Deepak Chopra, *The Seven Spiritual Laws of Success: A Practical Guide to the Fulfillment of Your Dreams* (New York: New World Library, 1994), p. 4.

[6]Ibid., p. 3.

[7]Deepak Chopra, *Ageless Body, Timeless Mind: The Quantum Alternative to Growing Old* (New York: Harmony Books, 1993), p. 27.

[8]Andrew Weil, *Natural Health, Natural Medicine: A Comprehensive Manual for Wellness and Self-Care* (Boston: Houghton Mifflin, 1990), p. 150.

[9]Gary Zukav, *The Seat of the Soul* (New York: Simon & Schuster, 1990), p. 111.

[10]Ibid., p. 186.

[11]Deepak Chopra, quoted in Tal Brooke, "Deepak Chopra—Wizard of Boundless

Healing," *SCP Journal* 21, no. 3 (1997): 13.

[12]Zukav, *Seat of the Soul*, p. 43.

[13]Marilyn Ferguson, *The Aquarian Conspiracy: Personal and Social Transformation in the 1980s* (Los Angeles: J. P. Tarcher, 1980), p. 381.

[14]Ibid.

[15]Ibid.

[16]Ibid., p. 315.

[17]Margot Adler, *Drawing Down the Moon: Witches, Druids, Goddess-Worshippers and Other Pagans in America Today* (Boston: Beacon Press, 1979), p. 23.

[18]Ibid., p. 175.

[19]Ibid., p. 25.

[20]Philip G. Davis, *Goddess Unmasked: The Rise of Neopagan Feminist Spirituality* (Dallas: Spence, 1998), p. 97.

[21]Ibid., p. 352.

[22]Peter Kreeft, *A Refutation of Moral Relativism: Interviews with an Absolutist* (San Francisco: Ignatius, 1999), p. 149.

[23]The Berkeley group is called Straight Edge, and the environmental group is called ELF, standing for Earth Liberation Front. On the latter, see "Vandals Target SUVs in Virginia," *Washington Times*, November 4, 2002, B-1.

Chapter 10: Consequences of the Denial

[1]Jean-Paul Sartre, mentioned in Francis Schaeffer, *Escape from Reason* (Downers Grove, Ill.: InterVarsity Press, 1968), p. 88. No exact quote or reference is given.

[2]Bertrand Russell, "A Free Man's Worship," quoted in William Lane Craig, *Apologetics: An Introduction* (Chicago: Moody Press, 1984), p. 46.

[3]Ludwig Wittgenstein, *Philosophical Review*, January 1965, quoted in John Montgomery, *The Suicide of Christian Theology* (Minneapolis: Bethany Fellowship, 1970).

[4]Jacques Derrida, "Force of Law: The Mystical Foundation of Authority," in *Deconstruction and the Possibility of Justice*, ed. Drucilla Cornell, Michel Rosenfeld and David Gray Carlson (New York: Routledge, 1992), pp. 14–15.

[5]Blaise Pascal, *Pensées*, trans. Alban Krailsheimer (New York: Viking, 1966), p. 247.

[6]G. K. Chesterton, *Autobiography*, quoted in G. K. Chesterton, *As I Was Saying: A Chesterton Reader*, ed. Robert Knille (Grand Rapids, Mich.: Eerdmans, 1985), p. 265.

[7]Steve Turner, "Creed," in *Up to Date* (London: Hodder and Stoughton, 1985), pp. 138–39.

[8]C. S. Lewis, *The Abolition of Man; or, Reflections on Education with Special Reference to*

the Teaching of English in the Upper Forms of School (Oxford: Collier, 1947), pp. 87–88.

[9]Aldous Huxley, *Ends and Means* (London: Chatto and Windus, 1938), pp. 270–73.

Chapter 11: Relativism Self-Destructs

[1]The statement "there are no moral absolutes" is not self-refuting but is wrong for other reasons given in this book.

[2]William Dembski, "The Fallacy of Contextualism," in *Unapologetic Apologetics: Meeting the Challenges of Theological Studies,* ed. William A. Dembski and Jay Wesley Richards (Downers Grove, Ill.: InterVarsity Press, 2001), p. 47.

[3]D. A. Carson, *The Gagging of God: Christianity Confronts Pluralism* (Grand Rapids, Mich.: Zondervan, 1996), p. 121.

[4]Dr. Jeffery Schloss, professor of biology, Westmont College, in a personal interview, August 2002.

[5]Richard Rorty, quoted in Carson, *Gagging of God,* p. 110.

[6]Barbara Johnson, translator's introduction, in Jacques Derrida, *Dissemination,* trans. Barbara Johnson (Chicago: University of Chicago Press, 1981), p. x.

[7]Jacques Derrida, *Writing and Difference,* trans. Alan Bass (Chicago: University of Chicago Press, 1978), pp. 280–81.

[8]C. S. Lewis, "Bulverism," in *First and Second Things: Essays on Theology and Ethics,* ed. Walter Hooper (Glasgow: Collins, 1985), p. 16.

[9]Watch the news or read the paper and see how often name-calling is preferred to argument.

[10]Lewis, "Bulverism," p. 17.

[11]Dorothy L. Sayers, "Selections from the Pantheon Papers," in *The Whimsical Christian: 18 Essays* (New York: Collier, 1987), pp. 8–9.

[12]C. S. Lewis, *Surprised by Joy: The Shape of My Early Life* (New York: Harcourt Brace, 1984), pp. 207–8.

[13]C. S. Lewis, "On the Reading of Old Books," in *First and Second Things,* pp. 27–28.

[14]Lewis, "Bulverism," p. 14.

[15]See, for instance, Ronald Nash, *The Concept of God* (Grand Rapids, Mich.: Zondervan, 1983); Richard Swinburne, *The Coherence of Theism* (Oxford: Clarendon, 1977); and Alvin Plantinga, *God, Freedom and Evil* (New York: Macmillan, 1968).

Chapter 12: Everybody's Right and Nobody's Right

[1]These distinctions are drawn from a helpful book by Mortimer Adler, *Truth in Religion: The Plurality of Religions and the Unity of Truth* (New York: Collier, 1990).

[2]J. I. Packer, foreword to *Reflections on Francis Schaeffer,* ed. Ronald W. Ruegsegger (Grand Rapids, Mich.: Zondervan, 1986), p. 14.

[3]C. S. Lewis, *"De Futilitate,"* in C. S. Lewis, *Christian Reflections,* ed. Walter Hooper (Grand Rapids, Mich.: Eerdmans, 1967), p. 65.

[4]See A. C. Graham, *Later Mohist Logic, Ethics and Science* (Hong Kong: Chinese University Press, 1978).

[5]See Philip J. Ivanhoe, "Mozi Chapter 35: Condemnation of Fatalism," in *Readings in Classical Chinese Philosophy,* ed. Philip J. Ivanhoe and Bryan W. Van Norden (New York: Seven Bridges Press, 2001), pp. 55, 57, 106.

[6]Li Hsaeh-Chin, *A Short History of Chinese Philosophy* (Beijing: Foreign Languages Press, 1959), pp. 12ff.

[7]Derrick Jensen, *A Language Older Than Words* (New York: Context Books, 2000), p. 63. See also Robert Dunkle, *The Classical Origins of Western Culture* (Brooklyn, N.Y.: Brooklyn College Press, 1986). I am indebted to Mike Marshall, now a Ph.D. candidate in philosophy, for pointing me to these sources in Chinese philosophy and on Sophism as well as his providing me a summary of their ideas.

[8]See David K. Clark and Norman L. Geisler, *Apologetics in the New Age: A Christian Critique of Pantheism* (Grand Rapids, Mich.: Baker, 1990), pp. 30–31.

[9]From a lecture at Cedar Point Farm. These themes are also contained in Os Guinness, *The Dust of Death: A Critique of the Establishment and the Counterculture, and the Proposal for a Third Way* (Downers Grove, Ill.: InterVarsity Press, 1972).

[10]V. K. Gokak, *Bhagavan Sri Sathya Baba* 216, quoted in Vishal Mangalwadi, *The World of Gurus* (New Delhi: Nivedit Good Books Distributors, 1987), p. 253.

[11]See Mangalwadi, *World of Gurus,* p. 260.

[12]Sarvepalli Radhakrishnan, *Indian Philosophy,* 1:180–86; cited in Clark and Geisler, *Apologetics in the New Age,* p. 60.

[13]See Ralph McInerny, *Aquinas Against the Averroists: On There Being Only One Intellect* (West Lafayette, Ind.: Purdue University Press, 1993).

Chapter 13: No Room for Evil

[1]C. S. Lewis, *Surprised by Joy: The Shape of My Early Life* (New York: Harcourt Brace, 1984), p. 65.

[2]C. S. Lewis, *Mere Christianity* (New York: Touchstone, 1996), pp. 45–46.

[3]Ibid., p. 19.

[4]C. S. Lewis, *The Abolition of Man; or, Reflections on Education with Special Reference to the Teaching of English in the Upper Forms of School* (Oxford: Collier, 1947), p. 42.

[5]Arthur Allen Leff, "Unspeakable Ethics, Unnatural Law," *Duke Law Journal,* December 1979, pp. 1229–30.

[6]Ibid., p. 1229.

[7]Ibid., p. 1230.

[8]Ibid., p. 1231.

[9]Ibid., p. 1232.

[10]Ibid., p. 1236.

[11]Ibid., p. 1240.

[12]Robert Nozick, quoted in ibid.

[13]Richard Posner, quoted in ibid., pp. 1242–43.

[14]Ibid., p. 1249.

[15]Arthur Koestler, *The Lotus and the Robot* (New York: Harper & Row, 1960), pp. 273–74, quoted in Pat Means, *The Mystical Maze* (Campus Crusade for Christ, 1976), p. 63.

[16]Richard Rorty, "Wild Orchids and Trotsky," in *Wild Orchids and Trotsky: Messages from American Universities,* ed. Mark Edmundson (New York: Penguin, 1993), p. 44.

[17]Richard Rorty, "Human Rights, Rationality and Sentimentality," in *The Human Rights Reader,* ed. Walter Laqueur and Barry Rubin (New York: New American Library, 1993), p. 266.

[18]James Miller, *The Passion of Michel Foucault* (Cambridge: Harvard University Press, 1993), p. 384.

[19]Ibid.

[20]Acharya Rajneesh, *Beyond and Beyond* (Bombay: Jeevan Jagruti Kendra, 1970), cited in Vishal Mangalwadi, *The World of Gurus* (New Delhi: Nivedit Good Books Distributors, 1987), p. 159.

[21]Yun-Men, quoted in Os Guinness, *The East, No Exit* (Downers Grove, Ill.: InterVarsity Press, 1974), p. 40.

[22]Herman Hesse, *Siddhartha,* trans. Hilda Rosner (New York: New Directions, 1951), p. 116.

[23]"13 Principles," *Principles of Wiccan Belief,* adopted by Council of American Witches, Spring 1974 Witchmeet, April 11–14, Minneapolis, from *Green Egg,* Box 1542, Ukiah, CA 95482.

[24]Erica Jong, *Witches* (New York: Harry N. Abrams, 1981), p. 52, cited in *Christian Research Journal,* summer 1990, p. 26.

[25]Starhawk, *The Spiral Dance: A Rebirth of the Ancient Religion of the Great Goddess* (San

Francisco: Harper & Row, 1979), pp. 80, 29.

[26]Alistair Crowley, cited in Margot Adler, *Drawing Down the Moon: Witches, Druids, Goddess-Worshippers and Other Pagans in America Today* (Boston: Beacon Press, 1979), p. 99.

Chapter 14: Truth That Transforms

[1]C. S. Lewis, "Is Theology Poetry?" in *The Weight of Glory and Other Literary Addresses* (San Francisco: HarperCollins, 1976), p. 106.

Recommended Books

Relativism and Postmodernism

Adler, Mortimer. *Truth in Religion: The Plurality of Religions and the Unity of Truth.* New York: Collier, 1990. An account of Adler's move from paganism to theism, rejecting relativism and pantheism along the way. He later became a Christian.

Beckwith, Francis J., and Gregory Koukl. *Relativism: Feet Firmly Planted in Mid-Air.* Grand Rapids: Baker, 1998. A short critique of relativism and analysis of how it has influenced American society.

Budziszewski, J. *What We Can't Not Know.* Dallas: Spence, 2003. A fascinating argument for common moral sense.

———. *Written on the Heart: The Case for Natural Law.* Downers Grove, Ill.: InterVarsity Press, 1997. An exposition of what natural law teaches us.

Carson, D. A. *The Gagging of God: Christianity Confronts Pluralism.* Grand Rapids, Mich.: Zondervan, 1996. A thorough examination of postmodernism, pluralism and inclusivism.

Copan, Paul. *True for You, but Not for Me: Defeating the Slogans That Leave Christians Speechless.* Minneapolis: Bethany House, 1998. An introduction to how we can address cultural objections to faith.

Erickson, Millard. *Postmodernizing the Faith: Evangelical Responses to the Challenge of Postmodernism.* Grand Rapids, Mich.: Baker, 1998. An excellent, thought-provoking study of varying evangelical interactions with postmodernism.

———. *Truth or Consequences.* Downers Grove, Ill.: InterVarsity Press, 2001. The best book yet in providing a readable and thorough survey of postmodernism and how to address it.

Gaede, Stan. *When Tolerance Is No Virtue.* Downers Grove, Ill.: InterVarsity Press, 1993. A balanced response to political correctness and multiculturalism.

Groothius, Douglas. *Truth Decay.* Downers Grove, Ill.: InterVarsity Press, 2000. A guide to understanding the different views of truth people hold and how to give a biblical response to them.

Guinness, Os. *Time for Truth: Living Free in a World of Lies, Hype, and Spin.* Grand Rapids, Mich.: Baker, 2000. A readable survey of the dilemma of truth in our age. Many excellent examples are given.

Kreeft, Peter. *A Refutation of Moral Relativism: Interviews with an Absolutist.* San Francisco: Ignatius Press, 1999. An imaginary dialogue with many helpful insights and quotes.

Lehman, David. *Signs of the Times: Reconstruction and the Fall of Paul deMan.* New York: Poseiden, 1991. A brilliant, fascinating look at postmodernism, the scandal surrounding one of its leaders, Paul deMan, and the movement's struggle to respond to it.

Lundin, Roger. *The Culture of Interpretation: Christian Faith and the Postmodern World.* Grand Rapids, Mich.: Eerdmans, 1993. A well-written book on the roots and fruits of postmodern literary theory.

McCallum, Dennis, ed. *The Death of Truth.* Minneapolis: Bethany House, 1996. A helpful collection of essays on the impact of postmodernism on various arenas of life, such as healthcare, education, literature, history, law and science.

McDowell, Josh, and Bob Hostetler. *The New Tolerance: How a Cultural Movement Threatens to Destroy You, Your Faith and Your Children.* Wheaton, Ill.: Tyndale House, 1998. One of the few books that helpfully takes on the tolerance held in our culture.

McGrath, Alister. *A Passion for Truth: The Intellectual Coherence of Evangelicalism.* Downers Grove, Ill.: InterVarsity Press, 1996. Helpful for evaluating postliberalism, postmodernism and pluralism.

Middleton, J. Richard, and Brian J. Walsh. *Truth Is Stranger Than It Used to Be: Biblical Faith in a Postmodern Age.* Downers Grove, Ill.: InterVarsity Press, 1995. Many helpful insights, leaning toward a positive response to postmodernism; see Millard Erickson's *Postmodernizing the Faith* for a helpful summary of the pros and cons of this book's position.

Murray, Michael J., ed. *Reason for the Hope Within.* Grand Rapids, Mich.: Eerdmans, 1999. Many helpful essays; see particularly chapters 7 and 8, on religious pluralism and Eastern religions.

Norris, Christopher. *Against Relativism: Philosophy of Science, Deconstruction, and Critical Theory.* Oxford: Blackwells, 1997. A good refutation of postmodern attempts to use science to support their position.

Oden, Thomas C. *After Modernity, What? Agenda for Theology.* Grand Rapids, Mich.: Zondervan, 1992. A brilliant look at how formerly liberal Thomas Oden now views the modernism he once held.

Phillips, Timothy R., and Dennis L. Okholm, eds. *Christian Apologetics in the Postmodern World.* Downers Grove, Ill.: InterVarsity Press, 1995. Helpful insights from a wide range of essays on how to shape apologetics in a postmodern world.

Schaeffer, Francis. *The God Who Is There*. Downers Grove, Ill.: InterVarsity Press, 1968. A must-read classic for today's generation. The task he calls us to is not completed.

Sproul, R. C., John Gerstner, and Arthur Lindsley. *Classical Apologetics: A Rational Defense of the Christian Faith and a Critique of Presuppositionalism*. Grand Rapids, Mich.: Zondervan, 1984. Help for formulating the case for absolutes. The book gives reasons for a belief that there is a God and for the authority of Scripture.

Veith, Gene Edward, Jr. *Postmodern Times: A Christian Guide to Contemporary Thought and Culture*. Wheaton, Ill.: Crossway, 1994. A good introductory survey of postmodernism.

White, James Emery. *What Is Truth?* Nashville: Broadman & Holman, 1994. A look at the concepts of truth held by American evangelicals such as Cornelius Van Til, Francis Schaeffer, Carl Henry, Donald Bloesch and Millard Erickson.

Zacharias, Ravi. *Jesus Among Other Gods: The Absolute Claims of the Christian Message*. Nashville: Word, 2000. A winsome discussion of Christianity's relation to other religions by a great communicator.

New Age and Neo-Paganism

Albrecht, Mark. *Reincarnation: A Christian Appraisal*. Downers Grove, Ill.: InterVarsity Press, 1982. An excellent source for a biblical response to reincarnation.

Chandler, Russell. *Understanding the New Age*. Dallas: Word, 1988. A good survey of New Age spirituality up to 1988.

Clark, David K., and Norman L. Geisler. *Apologetics in the New Age: A Christian Critique of Pantheism*. Grand Rapids, Mich.: Baker, 1990. A great philosophical critique of pantheism.

Copleston, Fredrick. *Religion and the One: Philosophies East and West*. New York: Crossroad, 1982. An outstanding philosophical discussion of the All is One philosophy.

Davis, Philip G. *Goddess Unmasked. The Rise of Neopagan Feminist Spirituality*. Dallas: Spence, 1998. An outstanding recent book on neo-paganism.

Geisler, Norman L., and J. Yutaka Anano. *The Reincarnation Sensation*. Wheaton, Ill.: Tyndale House, 1986. A survey of the issue of reincarnation.

Groothius, Douglas. *Confronting the New Age: How to Resist a Growing Religious Movement*. Downers Grove, Ill.: InterVarsity Press, 1988. A guide for confronting the New Age for readers with some understanding of the movement.

————. *Revealing the New Age Jesus: Challenges to Orthodox Views of Christ*. Downers Grove, Ill.: InterVarsity Press, 1990. Necessary reading that shows how New Age authors try to incorporate a different Jesus into their views.

Hoyt, Karen, ed. *New Age Rage*. Old Tappan, N.J.: Revell, 1987. Helpful insights into various dimensions of the New Age movement. My chapter is the last.

Jones, Peter. *Pagans in the Pews*. Ventura, Calif.: Regal, 2001. A revision and update of his earlier book *Spirit Wars* that shows how neopaganism has infiltrated the church.

Mangalwadi, Vishal. *The World of Gurus*. New Delhi, India: Nivedit Good Books, 1987. A superb response to Hinduism from an articulate believer in India.

Miller, Eliot. *A Crash Course in the New Age: Describing and Evaluating a Growing Social Force*. Grand Rapids, Mich.: Baker, 1989. A good introduction to the New Age way of thinking.

Newport, John P. *The New Age Movement and the Biblical Worldview: Conflict and Dialogue*. Grand Rapids, Mich.: Eerdmans, 1998. A very thorough update on New Age thinking and neo-paganism.

Zacharias, Ravi. *The Lotus and the Cross: Jesus Talks with Buddha*. Sisters, Ore.: Multnomah Publishers, 2001. A creative imagined dialogue between Jesus and Buddha. Zacharias spent considerable time researching this book by talking with Buddhist monks. It is very helpful in getting to the roots, questions and problems with this significant influence on the New Age Movement in the West.